IRANIAN SOCIETY

IRANIAN SOCIETY

An Anthology of Writings
by
JALAL AL-e AHMAD

Compiled and Edited
by
MICHAEL C. HILLMANN

MAZDA PUBLISHERS
P.O. BOX 136, LEXINGTON, KENTUCKY 40501 U.S.A.

Book No. 3
Iran-e No **Literary Collection**
Ahmad Jabbari: General Editor
Robert Olson: Consulting Editor

Partial funding for this volume was provided by
Amir Kabir Institute of Iranian Studies

ISBN: 0-939214-03-2
Library of Congress Catalog Card Number: 81-84761

Cover and book design by Ahmad Jabbari
Typesetting by TypeSetters, Lexington, Kentucky 40504
Printed by Colonial Press, Covington, Kentucky 41011

CONTENTS

PREFACE

This anthology of representative stories and essays by Jalal Al-e Ahmad (1923-1969) presents an Iranian view of Iranian society by a prominent contemporary writer as well equipped as any other post-World War II Iranian intellectual to describe and analyze that society. Al-e Ahmad began his writing career during the war years when the Allied Occupation of Iran taught a bitter lesson to those Iranians for whom the terms (neo-) colonialism, imperialism, and nationalism had meaning. After the war, Al-e Ahmad played an active role in politics, including membership in the Tudeh Communist Party. He was active in politics again during the turbulent Mosaddeq years from 1951 through 1953. Then, from late 1953 till his death in 1969, Al-e Ahmad was a leading social critic and spokesperson for the non-establishment Iranian intelligentsia *vis-à-vis* the Pahlavi regime, with unequivocal positions on foreign affairs, modernization and westernization, the American presence in Iran, the Iranian educational system, agriculture and land reform, the importance of religion in society, Iranian nationalism, and the like. In short, speaking from a perspective of personal experience of the great events from the beginning of World War II onward, Al-e Ahmad voices views of potentially special importance because his life spanned and writings encompass the cultural and social issues, conflicts, and dilemmas that thinking Iranians have been obliged to confront on a day-to-day basis for over forty years.

Iranian Society as this volume's title is not the product of an editor's imagination. It is precisely what Al-e Ahmad perceived as his primary focus of attention in all his essays from "The Hedayat of 'The Blind Owl'" (1951) to *On The Services and Disservices of Intellectuals* (1968). But his fifty or so short stories and four published longer works of fiction may be as validly subsumed under the heading "Iranian Society" because nearly all of Al-e Ahmad's fictional writings draw from a world not of the author's imagination but from an everyday contemporary Iranian world that the author has obviously experienced. Many of these stories, such as "My Sister and the Spider" (selection 2) and "The Pilgrimage" (selection 3), seem autobiographical in large part. And the purpose in most of them seems obviously not the effecting of reader aesthetic pleasure or the appreciation of some philosophical point, but rather criticism of or insight into specific aspects of contemporary Iranian society.

Iranian Society looks at Iranian society essentially through sketches of scenes and events and through the eyes of individuals involved in everyday affairs. Naturally, the most important individual depicted and represented is Al-e Ahmad himself, presented in his own words in "An Autobiography of Sorts" (selection 1) and "First Day at Mecca" (selection 14). Views of him by his widow Simin Daneshvar and younger brother Shams Al-e Ahmad are presented in the "Epilogue" (selection 16). And the same real life persona is very much a part of the autobiographical stories cited above, whose narrators seem to be Al-e Ahmad as a boy and young man respectively.

Two other prominent contemporary individuals are also depicted from Al-e Ahmad's perspective in this volume: Nima Yushij (1895-1960), the founder of the modernist trend in Persian poetry, in "The Old Man Was Our Eyes" (selection 11); and Samad Behrangi (1939-1968), the influential Azarbayjani folklorist and educational and social reformer, in "Samad and the Folk Legend" (selection 15). In "A Principal's First Day at School" (selection 9), Al-e Ahmad paints a portrait of another Iranian individual type, and the teachers and students at an elementary school seen from the principal's point of view. The girl in "The Sin" (selection 7), the pathetic rejected wife in "The Unwanted Woman" (selection 6), and the Tehran bazaar family in "The Untimely Breaking of the Fast" (selection 5) are other fictionalized Iranian individuals scrutinized by Al-e Ahmad in this volume.

The situations depicted are equally culture-specific and everyday: a group of people on a Tehran city bus in "The China Flowerpot" (selection 4), the annual Ramazan fast incumbent on Iranian Moslems in "The Untimely Breaking of the Fast" (selection 5), life at a presumably typical elementary school in "A Principal's First Day at School" (selection 9), the traditional pilgrimage to the Shi'i shrines in Karbala, Iraq, in "The Pilgrimage" (selection 2), and a *rowzeh* or prayer meeting held at a traditional middle class urban home in "The Sin" (selection 7).

Subjects and issues treated include western influence in Iranian higher education (selection 13), a 1960s look at the state of the craft of modernist Persian literature (selection 10), and a view, of course unaided by the hindsight of the civil upheaval of 1978 and after, of Iran's ultimate fate in the "Epilogue" (selection 16).

As piece-meal as the volume's representation of Iranian society may be, the view it presents is both comprehensive and reflective of perennially important social issues. The primary purpose of the volume is just that: to present Iranian society from an Iranian perspective that emphasizes that society's complexity and dilemmas.

Iranian Society has a secondary purpose as well. Even though primarily an anthology of translations, it is intended as a step toward appreciation of Al-e Ahmad's place as a contemporary Iranian literary artist and social critic by, if nothing else, providing an indication of the breadth of his interests and concerns as well as an unambiguous glimpse at his perspective and views. This volume is an initial step in this regard because serious study of Al-e Ahmad has yet to begin either in Iran or abroad.

In English, the single volume on Al-e Ahmad, John K. Newton's translation of Al-e Ahmad's popular short novel *The School Principal* (1958) is out of print. For more information about the volume, see "A Principal's First Day at School" (selection 9). Then, there are only two, overly brief, relatively reliable biobibliographical introductions to Al-e Ahmad in English, one in *Major Voices in Contemporary Persian Literature—Literature East and West* 20 (1976): 61-64, and the other in *Encyclopaedia of Islam: New Edition*, Supplement 1 (1980): 60-61. Both cite the available scattered and anthologized translations of Al-e Ahmad stories and essays, as well as the few critical studies of his works. Among the latter, "Al-e Ahmad's Fictional Legacy," *Iranian Studies* 9 (1976): 248-265, is the only relatively detailed treatment and refers to available Persian sources on the subject. Al-e Ahmad's place in contemporary Persian literature is discussed in passing in "Revolution, Islam, and Contemporary Persian Literature," *Iran: Essays on a Revolution in the Making* (Lexington: Mazda, 1981), pp. 121-142.

On the Persian side of things, some potentially significant writings by Al-e Ahmad remain unpublished, according to Simin Daneshvar. These include his diaries from 1946 through 1953, which were confiscated by the Pahlavi regime and perhaps destroyed, and extant handwritten diaries for the 1953 to 1969 years. Then there are numerous letters from 1949 to the end of his life. Many have been collected by the executors of Al-e Ahmad's estate, but many still remain in the hands of correspondents despite requests from the executors for copies. There are also extensive notes extant for a history of protest in Iran, which Al-e Ahmad planned to use in a volume treating the lives and views of Iranian dissidents and revolutionaries throughout history. In fiction, a novel

called *A Stone on a Grave* remains unpublished, as does a collection
of stories called *The New Generation*, although the posthumously
published *Five Stories* (1971) was apparently intended by Al-e
Ahmad to be part of that volume.

An important factor inhibiting serious study of Al-e Ahmad was
the inaccessibility of many of his works during the final decade of
Pahlavi rule. Among nearly thirty published works, no more than a
dozen or so were available at any one time from Al-e Ahmad's death
in September 1969 till 1978. Also, a number of works published in
those years appeared in censored editions. Four of his most important works: *The Letter 'N' and the Pen* (1961), *Weststruckness*
(1962), *Lost in the Crowd* (1961), and *The Cursing of the Land*
(1968), were never readily available to Iranian readers in the Pahlavi
era and, except for *Weststruckness*, are still little read. The first complete edition of *On the Services and Disservices of Intellectuals* did
not appear till 1978.

Furthermore, a politically dictated partial silence on Al-e
Ahmad's life and works commenced with his death, resulting in a
hiatus of serious discussion in Iran during most of the 1970s. Earlier,
there had been a promising beginning to critical appraisal with
Andisheh va Honar 5, no. 4 (1964): 344-489, although Al-e Ahmad
expressed great irritation at and disagreement with the critical essays
in *One Well and Two Pits* (1964). In the early and middle 1970s
there were only brief commemorative pages and essays in *Ettela'at,
Ferdowsi,* and the like. Then, there appeared a commemorative sec
tion and cover picture in *Javan,* no. 27 (1979): 24-35. Al-e Ahmad
received attention shortly thereafter in Mohammad 'Ali Sepanlu's
essay called "The Rise of the Novel in Iran," *Ketab-e Jom'eh* 1, nos
13, 14, and 15 (1979). Then came the special commemorative section on Al-e Ahmad in *Arash,* no. 31 (Sept./Oct. 1981): 47-98,
featuring pieces by Simin Daneshvar, Ahmad Shamlu, Ne'mat Mir-
zazadeh, Daryush Ashuri, and others. Feraydun Adamiyat's 22-page
pamphlet *Confusion in Historical Thinking* (1981) is the most
notable example of post-Pahlavi negative criticism of Al-e Ahmad.

That some of Al-e Ahmad's writing remains unpublished, that
some published writing was long banned or censored, and that
relatively little serious posthumous study has taken place are particularly lamentable facts because Al-e Ahmad was so much a man of
the Iranian present. This means, if it takes twenty or thirty years for
Al-e Ahmad's works to become known and the particulars of his life

and the views presented in his works to be studied and appreciated, in all likelihood the relevance of what he had to say will have diminished and he will be appreciated as a sterile, unthreatening phenomenon of the 1950s and 1960s, defused as it were through neglect. There is still time, however. For whatever decreasing relevance that might have been Al-e Ahmad's fate in almost any other sort of post-Pahlavi socio-political system is not the case with respect to the Islamic Republic of Iran that Ruhollah Khomeini, his supporters and followers, and the approval of the majority of Iran's urban population brought into existence during the spring of 1979. For the existence of the new Islamic state for a number of reasons makes particularly relevant much of Al-e Ahmad's commentary on the Iranian social and political order he was scrutinizing throughout his 25-year writing career.

First, Al-e Ahmad was raised in a family of Shi'ite clerics. As a product of this traditional urban Moslem family environment, Al-e Ahmad pays special attention to religion and society and offers a distinctive perspective in his writing to ongoing confrontations in Iran between past and present, traditions and change, religious values and secularism, Iranianness and westernization, and community and individual needs and prerogatives. As a result of his own family background and keen observation of people about him, Al-e Ahmad's works reflect views as specific and relevant to the Khomeini Islamic Republic as to the Pahlavi monarchy.

Secondly, Al-e Ahmad apparently came to believe that religious faith in Shi'i Islam was part and parcel of Iranianness and necessary to the survival of Iranian identity. In his widow's words:

> If he turned to religion, it was the result of his wisdom and insight because he had previously experimented with Marxism, socialism and, to some extent, existentialism, and his relative return to religion and the Hidden Imam was a way toward deliverance from the evil of imperialism and toward the preservation of national identity, a way toward human dignity, compassion, justice, reason, and virtue. Jalal had need of such a religion.

It may be that the dilemma Al-e Ahmad felt as an Iranian nationalist with modern ideas and a feeling for traditional religious values in the face of western influence has been resolved politically for the moment through the shift of the pendulum from wholesale Pahlavi westernization to theocratic isolation under Khomeini. However, in any attempt to discern existing alternatives within the poles of the Iranian political and social pendulum, Al-e Ahmad's remains a voice to reckon with.

Each of the sixteen selections in this volume is preceded by a short introductory note. These introductory notes provide full bibliographical citations for the original Persian selections being translated as well as background and other information pertinent to the selections. All Persian words and phrases in the volume are transliterated according to the system employed in *Hedayat's 'The Blind Owl' Forty Years After* (1978) and *Major Voices in Contemporary Persian Literature* (1980), except that no macron is herein used to distinguish between the /a/ of Tehran and the /a/ of Mashhad.

Michael C. Hillmann
Austin, Texas
December 1981

1

AN AUTOBIOGRAPHY OF SORTS

"Masalan Sharh-e Ahvalat" [An Autobiography of Sorts] was written in January 1968, some twenty months before Al-e Ahmad's death in September 1969 at the age of 46. Accounts of his last days and death are included in "Epilogue," selection 16.

"An Autobiography of Sorts" first appeared in the magazine *Jahan-e No* 24, no. 3 (1969): 4-8, and was reprinted in the posthumously published short story collection called *Panj Dastan* [Five Stories] (Tehran, 1971), as well as in subsequent commemorative features on Al-e Ahmad in several magazines through the 1970s. It was also reprinted in *Jalal Al-e Ahmad, Mardi dar Keshakesh-e Tarikh-e Mo'aser* [Jalal Al-e Ahmad, A Man in the Struggle of Contemporary History] (Tehran: Kaveh, 1978), a volume of critical essays and commemorative articles and poems compiled by Hamid Tabrizi.

Although names of people, organizations, and publications mentioned in "An Autobiography of Sorts" may be unfamiliar to readers not acquainted with contemporary Iranian history, the essay should still convey a clear sense of Al-e Ahmad's involvement in and commitment to Iranian society, as well as a feel for his personality and characteristic ways of looking at things. And what is left unsaid about society and politics in the essay should give the reader an impression of how pervasive and extensive censorship of writing was during most of the post-Mosaddeq pre-Khomeini era from 1953 to 1978.

I come from a religious, Shi'i Moslem family. My father, older brother, and one of my brothers-in-law died in religious dignity. And now I have a nephew and another brother-in-law in religion. And-that's only the beginning. Because the rest of the family is all religious too. With an exception here and there. Reflections of this religious environment can be observed in *The Exchange of Visits* (1946) and *Seh'tar* (1948) and throughout all my other drivel.

My glorious arrival into this zoo of a world took place in 1923. No exaggeration, I was the first boy after seven girls. None of whom, of course, were blind. But only four of them have survived. Two of them died of chicken-pox and diarrhea in childhood, and another died of cancer at age thrity-five. My childhood was spent in a sort of aristocratic religious affluence. Till Davar's Ministry of Justice decided to take over notary public offices and my father refused to knuckle under to the government's insignia and stamps and supervision; so he closed up shop and was content to be the neighborhood religious elder. When I finished elementary school, he didn't let me study further. He told me to go to work in the bazaar so that he could make me what he was. And I went to the bazaar, but I also secretly registered at Darolfonun, which had recently opened up night classes. I worked days repairing watches, then doing electrical wire lining, then selling leather goods and such things. And at night, school. And with a year's income from steady work, I finished the rest of high school. Thereafter as well, I occasionally did odd electrical wiring repairs. With my brother-in-law Javad who was an electrician. This is how high school got finished. And the title "graduate" was affixed to the certificate of my existence in 1943—that is to say, in war time. In such fashion a young man from that religious environment about 5'9" tall, with a carnelian ring and a shaved head was handed over to the confusions of World War II. A war that for us had no killing and destruction and bombs. But it had famine and typhus and chaos, and the painful presence of occupation forces.

When the war was over, I finished the Faculty of Letters (Teacher Training College). That was 1946. And I became a teacher. In 1947. In the meantime I had broken with my family. I had one necktie and one second-hand American suit which only God knows which soldier's body going to the warfront it came off of so that I could buy it for 70 tomans at Shamsol'emareh. By this time I had been a member of the Tudeh Party for three years. During the last years of high school, I became familiar with Ahmad Kasravi's works and speeches and *Payman* magazine and then *Mard-e Emruz* and *Tafrihat-e Shab*, and then *Donya* magazine and the publications of the Tudeh Party... and with this we had organized something on

Entezam Street in Amiriyeh called "Society of Reform." And at night free of charge we taught *le français* and Arabic and public speaking. And we had a daily bulletin that we tacked on walls. And for the purpose of looking into the work of political parties that were spreading like mushrooms, each of us were assigned to a specific party. And we visited their headquarters and attended their meetings...And I was assigned to the Tudeh Party. And on Fridays we'd gather and argue above Pasqal'eh and Kolakchal about who the good guys and who the traitors were and about what should be done, and the like...till finally we decided to join the Tudeh Party. As a group. Except for a couple who didn't join. And this was in the spring of 1944.

Other members of that Society of Reform were: Amir Hosayn Jahanbeglu, Reza Zanjani, Howshidar and 'Abbasi and Darabzand, 'Alinaqi Monzavi, and one or two others I don't recall. Before joining the Party, I had translated a pamphlet from Arabic under the title "Illegal Mournings" that was published in 1943. We sold them at two rials a copy and sold out in two days, and we were very happy that our Society had sponsored at least one profitable venture. Would you believe it that religious bazaar merchants bought them all on credit and then burned them! I found out about it later. Before this I had also written other nonsense on the reformation of religious ideas that remained unpublished and unpursued.

In the Tudeh Party in four years I rose from being a simple member to membership on the Tehran central committee. And during two of these years I constantly wrote. In "Bashar baraye Daneshjuyan" which I ran and in the monthly magazine *Mardom* which I edited. And occasionally in *Rahbar* as well. My first story appeared in *Sokhan*. The New Year's issue of 1945. *Sokhan* at that time was being published under the wings of Sadeq Hedayat and thus everyone there was obliged to lean toward the left. I published *The Exchange of Visits* in the winter of 1946. It was a collection of what had appeared in *Sokhan* and the weekly *Mardom baraye Rowshanfekran*. As a result of publishing all this stuff I was assigned in the spring of 1946 to launch *Mardom* under the supervision of Ehsan Tabari. I published eighteen issues altogether up to the split. For six months I even ran the Party's Sho'lehvar Press. Which after the defeat of the *Democrat Farqasi* and the damage the Party inflicted and the flight of its leaders had been moved from behind the broken down Opera Building to within the Party. And because of the power I had at the printing house the book *Our Suffering* appeared. In the fall of 1947.

Containing stories of defeat in those political battles told in socialist realist style! And the splintering of Tudeh in the late fall of 1947. As a consequence of this difference of opinion between a group that we constituted lead by Khalil Maleki and party leaders who because of the defeat on the Azarbayjan issue no longer controlled the general context of Party thought. And for this reason they followed Stalinist policies that we saw the results of. After the break, we organized a socialist party that wasn't able for long to withstand the Party media allegations that had even Radio Moscow behind them. And we disbanded and were obliged to keep quiet.

It was during this period of silence that I did some translations. With the aim of learning *le français*. I translated some from Gide, Camus, Sartre. And also Dostoyevski. Also from this period is the book *Seh'tar* which was dedicated to Khalil Maleki. Also during this period I got married. When one comes up short in the big world, you build a smaller one with the four walls of a house. Flight from the paternal home to the Society of the Party and from that to one's own home. And my wife is Simin Daneshvar, whom you know. A bibliophile and writer and professor of art and author and translator of many books. And in fact a sort of friend and helper for this pen of mine. If she weren't around, o how much nonsense would have flowed from this pen! (as if it has not occurred as it is!) And from 1950 till today nothing has been published under my name that Simin didn't read and critique before everyone else.

And everything pretty much stayed the same up to nationalization of oil and the appearance of the National Front and Dr. Mosaddeq. When I was pulled into politics again. And again for three more years a struggle. In handling *Shahed* and *Niru-ye Sevom* [Third Force] newspapers and *'Elm va Zendegi* whose editor was Maleki. In addition, I was the manager of the public relations section and a member of the Third Force committee which was part of *Jebheh-ye Melli* [National Front]. And so forth till the spring of 1953 when because of a difference of opinion with Third Force leadership, I withdrew to the sidelines. They wanted to fire Naser Vosuqi who was one of the party leaders. And with those same Beria tactics. Which I no longer was in the mood for. I mean it was because of these same shenanigans that we had split from the Tudeh Party. And once again they'd started.

During these years I translated Gide's *Return from Russia* and also *Contaminated Hands* by Sartre. Both for obvious reasons. *The*

Unwanted Woman also belongs to these years. My acquaintance with Nima Yushij dates from this period. And also the beginning of my fooling around with painting. The struggle that arose among us from within the National Front with the Tudeh Party in these three years was in my opinion one of the most productive years of intellectual growth and criticism.

Let's forget about the fact that the upshot of defeat in that struggle lay like sediment at our feet. The defeat of the National Front and the victory of the companies—which I talked about allegorically in *Adventure of the Beehives*—brought about a second enforced silence that proved an opportunity for a serious self-look and in the reasons for those defeats for getting exact about oneself. And travelling around the country. And its fruits: *Owrazan, The Tati Speakers of Boluk-e Zahra,* and *The Island of Kharg.* Afterwards, because of these books, the Social Research Institute of the Faculty of Letters at the University of Tehran wanted me to supervise their series of publications in this field. Thus it was that such monographs became one of their endeavors. However, after the publication of five monographs I left them. Because I saw that they wanted to make a commodity out of those monographs for European consumption and necessarily with European criteria. But I wasn't cut out for this sort of thing. Because my aim in such an endeavor was a renewal of self-awareness and a new assessment of the local environment and also with our own criteria. However, in any case, this field is still being pursued.

And this is how a young religious man who ran away from home and survived the confusion of war and its politics becomes aware of the essential contradictions of traditional Iranian social underpinings, watching western countries changing it to suit their needs and perhaps making another colony of it. These were the things that prompted *Weststruckness*—1962—which I had earlier rehearsed in *Three More Essays.* Before this I published *The School Principal*—1958—the results of personal reflection and immediate instinctive impressions of the small but extremely important realm of education and the school. But with direct allusions to general conditions of the day and these sorts of independence-shattering problems.

The publication of *Weststruckness* which was done secretly was a sort of turning point in my writing career. One of its symptoms was that the publication of *Kayhan-e Mah* was suspended. Which I had got going in the spring of 1962 and although it had the financial backing of the Kayhan Company behind it it didn't last more than six months and although it had a group of some fifty responsible and *engage* writers no more than two issues were published. Why? Because I had published the first chapter of *Weststruckness* in the very first issue, which prompted the interference of the censors and the necessity of tearing out those pages et cetera...

The gloom and distress resulting from this renewed enforced silence I eased through several trips that arose after this. To Europe in the fall of 1962 and winter of 1963. On assignment from the Ministry of Education and for the purpose of studying the publication of textbooks. A pilgrimage to Mecca in the spring of 1964. To Russia that summer with an invitation to participate in the Seventh International Congress of Anthropology. And to America in the summer of 1965. At the invitation of Harvard University for an international literature and political science seminar. And a travelogue resulted from each trip. The one for the pilgrimage was published with the title *Lost in the Crowd.* And the one for Russia was being published in serial fashion in a literary weekly Shamlu and Ro'ya'i were putting out. Then once again the censors intervened and closed down the weekly. I also published a short report on the Anthropology Congress in *Payam-e Novin* and another short report on the Harvard trip in *Jahan-e No* which Dr. Baraheni was editing, and once again they didn't put up with more than four issues of our stuff. It was in this journal that I published two chapters of *On the Services and Disservices of Intellectuals.* That was in 1966. Prior to this, the book *Hasty Evaluation*, a collection of eighteen critical articles on contemporary society, literature, art, and politics, was printed in 1964 in Tabriz. And before that, the tale *The Letter 'N' and the Pen*, in 1961, which is written in an eastern folktale style, and in it deals with the hows and whys of the defeat of contemporary leftist movements.

The translation of *Rhinoceros* by Eugene Ionesco in 1966—and the publication of a complete translation of Ernest Younger's *Passing the Line* which had been prepared for *Kayhan-e Mah,* and was edited by Mohammad Human with two chapters having appeared in *Kayhan-e Mah.* And I've just gotten *The Cursing of the Land* published which is the story of a school teacher in a village during a nine-month period and what happens to him and the people of the village. With the purpose of having the final word on water and cultivation and the land and the policies which the government used to misdirect people such as water and cultivation and the confusion that necessarily took place. And also for the purpose of a different evaluation opposed to the politicians' and the government's concerning the sale of property which they called "Land Reform".

Hereafter I have to ready *On the Services and Disservices of Intellectuals* for the press. Which is the work of 1964/65 and now needs some editing. And then I have to finish the translation of "Thirst and Hunger," and then I have to rewrite *A Stone on a Grave* which is a story about parental childlessness. And then I've got to complete *The New Generation*, which is another story of another generation that I'm part of...and you see it is not only that businessman who invited you to his place one night at Kish Island. And what a melancholy mood he was in...

Translation by the editor

2

MY SISTER AND THE SPIDER

"Khaharam va 'Ankabut" [My Sister and the Spider] is one of a number of Al-e Ahmad stories that both seem obviously autobiographical and are narrated by a character who seems to be Al-e Ahmad as a boy. Another is "Jashn-e Farkhondeh" [The Joyous Celebration], first published in *Arash* 1, no 1. (Oct./Nov. 1961) and later reprinted in *Panj Dastan* [Five Stories] (Tehran, 1971) where "My Sister and the Spider" was also published.

"The Joyous Celebration," which has been translated by Minoo S. Southgate in *Modern Persian Short Stories* (Washington, D.C.: Three Continents, 1980), pp. 19-33, is a boy's description of his father's reaction to an invitation to a reception that he must attend with his wife. The story takes place shortly after Reza Pahlavi banned the wearing of the chador by women in 1936. And the father, who is a Shi'i cleric, instead of taking his wife, that is, the narrator's mother, makes arrangements with a military officer acquaintance for a *sigheh* or temporary marriage contract with the latter's daughter whom he will take to the reception as his wife.

"My Sister and the Spider" may strike many readers as not being as pointed as "The Joyous Celebration" in terms of social commentary. Still, there may be telling culture-specific implications in details of the relationships among family members. And some critics, including translator A. Reza Navabpour, see the story as an allegorical representation of the early 1950s' oil crisis, with the sister representing the Iranian people or Mosaddeq's government abandoned or ill treated by the West, the Tudeh Party, the bazaar, and the clergy.

I

I first saw it last week. One afternoon when my brother-in-law had come to see how his wife was. I spotted it when I was bringing him a cup of tea. Big, black and ugly. How gross! You could even see its hairs from that distance. It had spun a large web in the top corner by the window, behind the glass. Spreading from three corners of the window. Eight small black balls were suspended in it, here and there. Pity the flies. While my brother-in-law was taking his sugar lumps, I counted the corpses once again. There were exactly eight. How had I failed to notice such a large spider before? I, who knew even the smallest ant hole, and was aware of when all the mice gave birth.

Of course it wasn't surprising that my mother hadn't seen it, despite the scrupulousness with which she swept and cleaned. This last month she always had one foot in the kitchen, and the other by my sister's bed. The demands of my father and his visitors carried on as usual. Yet nobody else had the right to touch my sister's bed.

It was the first time that the sick bed had come to our house. Her husband had brought it from their own house. We put the bed by the window, and my sister always slept on it. To tell the truth she didn't sleep, she was bedridden. Initially it seemed to me that she was spoiled, because sometimes she walked into the yard. She would get as far as the pool to wash her hands and face. But as soon as her husband knocked at the door, she would run and jump into bed. Actually she didn't run, she walked quickly, and lay down. But now it has been a month since she became paralyzed. I say that because sometimes I had to empty the bed pan which was left under her bed. What a smell!

When I had taken the tea tray back, I went and got my ruler from my bookshelf, and went after the spider. My sister had again started to moan and groan by the time I arrived. I put one foot on the edge of the bed, and one hand on the wall, and I was about to aim my ruler at the spider's web with my other hand, when my brother-in-law shouted, "Old man, don't you know she aches in every bone?"

Although the bed creaked under my foot, I knew it was not that easy to break it. I wasn't going to harm my sister. Nevertheless I didn't say anything. I glanced at her and saw the pain in her face. She said nothing herself, only closed her eyes, stretched her neck and flared her nostrils. Her forehead was full of wrinkles. Then I was sorry, and I climbed down. The ruler weighed heavily in my hand as I heard myself say, "Well—I wanted to kill this filth."

My sister opened her eyes and asked, "Why?"

"Why not, sister? Mother says that spiders bring bad luck. Anyway don't you see how many flies he's caught?"

Her husband said, "It's the flies' own fault, old man. They shouldn't be so nosy. He's sitting in his own house...."

Was he teasing me? I had never got on with this brother-in-law of mine. Ever since the start of their marriage, I mean my sister's wedding night. The bride was late getting ready, and the bridegroom's house was so chaotic and had so many corridors, porches and stairs that I was exhausted. Indeed my hands were dropping off. Carrying the mirror on your back for the whole way was something even the adults couldn't have done. When we arrived at the porch of the house, I don't know how it happened, but I fell over. I must have been looking at the vines which were hanging from the trellis. Suddenly I realized I was in the middle of the orange tree vase. The mirror broke. My hands and face were bleeding. I didn't know whether to cry or not when my brother-in-law came up, that is—the groom. Unmoved, he said, "Old man, were you dozing?" I burst into tears. From then on he called me 'old man.' But I wasn't the only one. No one ever got on with him. Every day at the table they moaned about him—that he had kept his wife as long as she was healthy, and now she was ill, he had brought her back to her mother and left her. This is why I paid no attention to him, and said, "What kind of grave does it live in? This filth has wormed his way into our house."

"Dear 'Abbas, I've done the same thing."

"You, sister?"

I didn't know what to say. What did she mean? Why should my sister compare herself with a spider? As soon as I asked myself this question, I realized that she was teasing her husband. I saw that I was in the way. I picked up her husband's empty glass and went out. I took him a waterpipe, and observed that he had calmed my sister. He was gently relating the tale of a haji who was their neighbor, and who had recently become a member of the Chamber of Commerce. Every day he had to wear a tie, but he didn't know how to tie it. The day before yesterday, early, he sent for my brother-in-law to go and tie it for him, and then they had been served breakfast. Now God was on his side, and he does it every day, and as his wife isn't there to make breakfast for him...and so on. I saw I had no patience for him. He was always telling these insipid stories. I had a feeling he was inventing them to keep my sister quiet. It was habitual. First they had discussions and quarrels, then they made up, and for an hour or two it was all pleasant chat. Then my brother-in-law would leave. Seven days a week. In the afternoons when I got back from school, neither my father nor my mother would face him. Either I or my younger sister opened the door for him. And I had to wait on him. Every day there were these tales. That's why I told myself I'd better get on with my work.

When I went out of the room, I drew up a plan of attack against the spider, "Filthy bastard! You should pray to the soul of my sister!"

And I went off to do my homework.

II

The math exam was close at hand, and I didn't know much of it. Especially since I had quarrelled with the math master, and had failed the second term. Once I was arranging my film book in class when he came and took it and threw it out of the window. He had just started wearing a European hat, and knew that my father was a mullah. He was always after me, and then at the time of the prohibition of the turbans he was after mullahs. He was always criticizing. He didn't even respect the religion teacher who after all was his colleague, and came to school in a turban. He wore it as he entered the classroom, but as soon as he sat at his desk, he took it off and put it on the desk, folded his robe, and put it on the turban. When the bell rang, he shook the chalk off the robe, threw it over his shoulders, placed the turban on his head, and stood up. At first we laughed at him, saying, "Preacher, your turban's fallen off," and so on. But later, we didn't bother him. But would the math teacher leave him alone? He was always carping and criticizing until in the end, when one day he was imitating the mullahs combing their beards, I stood up and straight to his face said, "What harm have the mullahs done to you? Stolen your cuckold father's money?"

And I ran out of the classroom. In fact I'd learnt this word "cuckold" from my father. I didn't even know what it meant, like *zendiq* and lots of other things. But I knew these things came out when my father got very heated.

I didn't go to math class any more. It was clear then that the failure was on my shoulders. The saving grace was that the final exam was external, and the principal had recommended me. He respected my father. Otherwise I would have been bound to fail.

I had either done alright in the other exams or was sure to do okay. But this math, especially percentages and proportions. When I opened that book it was as if someone was beating me. But what could I do? Wilting, I sat down beside my bookshelf and opened the book. "If there are 20 bales of cotton in a store and the volume of every bale...," I read.

But would the image of that great black spider leave me alone? I was sure I could have caught it if my sister hadn't always been in bed this last month. What a pity. Well, surely my sister can't have grown fond of it? How can she lie in bed all day and every day with that pain? Some nights you know she kept me awake as well with her cries, followed by the whispering of my mother as she begged her to take some medicine. There was a tray of medicine under the bed... How can she read prayer books all the time? With her level of knowledge—she was asking me about Sobhan and Mannan. Inevitably time and again she would gaze at the spider, watching his coming and going, hunting and swinging. That's what I tell myself. Look, can you sit still for a whole hour on the bench, watching the blackboard or the teacher's mouth? You think of a thousand things. Well how about a whole month lying in bed and doing nothing! Not able to...

When I thought a little, I realized that in this way I was getting rid of my hate for the spider. Suppose my sister has found a pastime with this spider, what is it to me? A spider is only a spider. My sister might like lots of other things. Like this husband. She's been with him for five or six years, and ill for all of it. No children, and several times had to go to hospital. Take me—do I like my brother-in-law? It's true I don't like flies either, but I wouldn't want even one fly in the whole world to fall into any spider's web. Lots of times on hot summer afternoons, so as to play a quiet game and not disturb my father's sleep, I caught flies, and put them at the edge of ant holes. But whenever I've seen one of these very flies trapped in a spider's web, I've not only freed it straight away but I've knocked down the spider, his nest and web as well. The problem is that when you release the flies which have been caught in the spider's web, they are no good anymore. I don't know why. Perhaps that's why I don't like spiders. When the fly is caught, it makes a kind of muffled buzzing. As if the noise comes from the bottom of its throat. It makes no difference being caught by ants or in the fingers of someone like me—who traps its legs and lets it helplessly flap its wings. But whenever its caught in the spider's web it's as though its voice is still more muffled. As if the spiders close the mouth of the fly so it can't call for help. Or throttle it...how should I know? Again, if you want the fly to be caught by ants, you must pluck off at least one wing so it won't fly. Or push a wood splinter up its ass so if it tries to fly, it can't. But it's not like this with a spider's web. The fly is flying safe and secure in the air when suddenly he's caught in the web. Just like a small ball in a volleyball net. Perhaps it doesn't see, or it's confused, or preoccupied. Indeed, is it possible to see the spider's web? It's so fine. Sometimes I don't see it myself. Then before it can do anything, the spider is there like suspended death. The trouble is that the flies don't take it seriously at first. I've noticed. They don't even make any noise. They shift about for a bit, and as soon as one of their wings or some of their legs are trapped and the spider has appeared, then they make a noise. If they spoke out sooner, perhaps someone like me would appear and come to their help. But the problem is that when the flies cry out, it's too late... I was thinking like this, and the book was open to page 32 when I felt my mother standing above me. She always moved silently. If you didn't have your wits about you you could say she was always everywhere in the house.

"What are you doing, love?"

"I'm doing my homework. This bloody math is enough to kill my father."

"Don't say that, love, it's not right. May the Lord protect him for you. You mustn't repeat what your elders say. Come along, go and get some bread. Your supper will be late."

I threw the book on the shelf and set off. I was putting on my shoes when my mother said, "Will you do me a favor?"

I just looked at her. My mother turned her face away and went towards the shelf to light the lamp. She didn't usually speak to me like this. At home I had to do what I was told. No questions asked and no hesitation. It's true that sometimes I complained, but that was mostly about my father's orders, which were difficult and given sternly, not about my mother's requests. So I stayed quiet. My mother struck the match, lit the lamp and replacing the funnel, said, "Tomorrow lunchtime, on your way back, pop in to Ostad Asghar's shop. He'll give you a handful of lead. Bring it home."

I saw there were tears in her eyes. I said, "Well mother, I've got exams tomorrow."

"What's the difficulty, love? They won't keep you for lunch. I'm asking for your sister's sake."

"My sister?"

"Yes dear. Can't you see how much pain she's in?"

"But what's lead got to do with my sister's illness?"

"Don't ask too many questions, love. The baker will be crowded. Hurry up, so you don't get caught in the rush."

Then suddenly my sister's cry rose from the upstairs room. One of those screams that would wake the dead. I couldn't stand it. It made your flesh creep. So I stopped persisting with my mother about the lead, and left. As I was coming out of the door I came face to face with the pharmacist's boy, who every evening came to inject my sister.

III

Lunchtime next day, returning from my exam, I was furious. I felt I'd messed it up—with that percentage and proportions. The exam question was neither about the cotton bale, nor the volume of the store. It was about the amount of water it was necessary to have in a watertrough to quench the thirst of a battalion's horses. If each horse drinks so much water, and the number of horses...this sort of rubbish. More significantly, I didn't understand what "watertrough" meant. I think we all messed it up. So on my way I was neither in the mood to quarrel with children I didn't know, nor to snatch fruit from the greengrocer on the corner of the street who'd just brought in the first red grapes. Apart from the fact that I would have had to change my route. I went through the back alleys of the Mo'ir Bazaar to Zir-e Gozar. When I arrived at the lead molder they had just finished their work, and were about to send the boy to get bread, yoghurt and kabobs for lunch. I said, "Hello," stepped over the row of molds, and went towards Ostad Asghar. I knew him. He was one of my father's followers. He never forgot to go to sermons or to the mosque. On sermon nights, he was always in charge of the samovar. He made such a good base for the teapots on the brazier, it was a pleasure to see. Red hot charcoal, like pomegranate flowers. And not the slightest smell or smoke. None at all! His goods were not part of our daily necessities like the grocer and butcher, where my father would send me every day to get things on credit, and sometimes to get cash. I would rather go and apologize to the math teacher instead and avoid these particular tasks. But would my father have any sympathy? He would bellow out his command, and while you were fumbling about being embarrassed or whatever, he would roar, "You little ass! Do you think I'm getting protection money from them?"

Anyway, it was the first time I had been to the lead molder's shop. Ostad Asghar returned my greeting, and said, "Haven't you brought a container with you?"

I said, "No."

So he called on one of the boys who went to the cellar and brought a bucket made from half a tin oil can. The handle was made of wire. Ostad Asghar himself, using a short handled shovel, took the metal pieces from the heap in the corner of the shop. While he was filling the bucket, I studied the rows of molds in the middle of the shop where the gleam of the metal drops on the sand were quite fresh, and around the drops the sand was dry. In the heat of the shop there was a smell which burnt the back of your throat and tasted acrid. When the bucket was full, Ostad Asghar picked it up, and handed it to me, saying, "Goodbye. Don't forget to return the bucket."

I took hold of the bucket—casually. It immediately fell. How did I know it was that heavy? The bottom of the bucket hit the toes of my right foot. It was agonizing. Two or three shop boys laughed heartily. I was so infuriated that I would have smashed their faces in if it had been after school hours. Ostad Asghar took the bucket, filled it up again with the metal pieces and placed it in front of me. "You're not hurt?" he said. "They call this lead. Be careful, son, it's heavy."

I was so embarrassed that I left without saying goodbye. It really was heavy. It weighed a ton. Maybe not a ton, but it was the heaviest weight that I had carried up till then. It seemed to me as if it weighed as much as the weight which every Friday the Dash-Mashdis in Execution Square used to bet on, and struggled to lift, while the veins in their necks stood out and their necks became like tree trunks. With biceps like fists under the skin. Only twenty paces from the shop, I realized I couldn't do it. It couldn't be treated lightly, not with one hand. My satchel was under my arm. My toes were really aching. I put the bucket down, and rubbed my toes through my cotton shoes.

When I had recovered I put my satchel on top of the lead, picked up the bucket in both hands, and set off. The bucket dangled awkwardly between my legs. I couldn't go fast like that. The bucket was swinging and hitting my legs. Every 20 paces I put the bucket down, regained my breath, rubbed my fingers where the sharp wire handle was cutting in and I carried on towards my house. But none of this was important. All the way I was wondering what was the connection between all this lead and my sister's illness. "A handful of lead," my mother had said. I had thought it could be carried in my pocket or in my satchel. And indeed, no one had asked me anything about it in the shop. As soon as I'd said, "Hello," they gave me the bucket and then that disaster had happened. Perhaps my mother had mentioned it to my father, and he had arranged it all with Ostad Asghar before he went to Qom, either last night, or at the morning prayers. I could see all this, and that's why I hadn't said anything. Anyway, if the bucket hadn't fallen on my foot and I hadn't made a fool of myself in front of the molder's boys, the whole business would have been forgotten. But not now. Why on earth must all this lead go to our house? I had heard that bullets were made of lead, but we had nothing to do with guns. Ah yes! Perhaps it was for making dumbbells like weightlifters use. I laughed and put the bucket down.

"Fool. You're always making an idiot of yourself. That stinking exam, then that disaster in front of the boys, and now...do you suppose that if your sister took up weightlifting she would be cured?..."

The main point was that I knew there was a connection between that heavy damned lead and my sister's illness. Then I suddenly remembered...Oh yes, that's it. "Dey put 'ot yead...dey put 'ot yead...."

The day before yesterday when Sanambar was leaving, she was muttering this to herself and laughing. I hadn't understood it at the time. Now I did. Sanambar was a crippled creature—beggarlike—who once a week came to our house, ate lunch, and left. She dragged one side of her body along the ground, and on her other side she carried a nose bag on her shoulder where she put whatever she came across. The horrid thing about her was that she dribbled all the time, and the clothes on her chest were always like a piece of leather, and her speech...how can I put it? The simplest things turned into a riddle, because she hardly pronounced any letter correctly. Her mouth was twisted and always full of spit, and you could hardly understand what she said at all. But now I did understand,

and to tell the truth, I was really angry to see that even Sanambar knew what was going on in our house and I didn't.

So, imitating my father—huffing and puffing—I came in the house and dropped the lead bucket noisily by the pool. I took off my jacket, then my shoes and socks, and put my foot in the pool. At first there were shooting pains in my toes, then they felt hot. They got better as I rubbed them in the cool water. Fish timidly approached my foot, and then fled. Watching them, I took care of my foot where the skin of my big toe and the two others next to it was grazed and swollen. It smarted as I touched it.

"Lord release me. Whatever have you done to yourself?" my mother said.

"Leave me alone, you don't care. Tell me, is this what you mean by a handful of lead?"

My mother sat on the edge of the pool, and examined my foot. Laughing she said, "Love, you're not fussy. You're acting like a girl. Did you think it was a sword cut?"

"I want to know what all this lead's for."

"You'll see, you'll see. May God save you from hell's fire. Get up now, your lunch will be cold."

She fetched her own towel and sat down to dry my foot. Again I noticed her eyes were full of tears. She was always like that, so you couldn't argue or get angry with her. So I put on my socks, splashed water on my face, and went in.

The table was well crowded. My mother's aunt was there with two of my elder sisters, and another woman who I didn't know. Her whole face was sagging, her chin, the tip of her nose, and even her cheeks and under her eyes and lips. I said hello and sat down. My plate was clearly fuller than usual. Lentil pilaw with raisins and dates. And what a crust! The raisins were burnt or swollen, and oily. Definitely no one could make a crust better than my mother.

I was busy eating when I heard, "It's getting a grip on her like a spider."

"Well Khambaji, it's not called cancer for nothing." My mother's aunt said this to the unknown woman. I didn't understand what "cancer" meant, but I pricked up my ears as the strange woman swallowed her mouthful and said, "So then what, cousin. Branding is for these situations."

Horrified, I looked up, as my mother gesticulated to the strange woman that I mustn't know. My mother's aunt, in order to change the subject, said, "My mother, God bless her, said hell's fire is forbidden for them."

I couldn't stand it any more. I ran upstairs after my sister. She was sitting in her bed eating her broth spoonful by spoonful. Her eyes were fixed on the spider in the corner of the window. I sat beside her bed, and sobbing, shouted, "What do they want to do to you, sister? I won't let them, sister, I won't allow it...."

Then my mother arrived. With her hand on my head, she said, "Dear boy, you are now grown up. She wanted it herself, didn't you, love?"

My sister threw the spoon on the tray, and shouted, "Oh God, why don't you give me death? Why?"

She was shouting like this as I ran out of the house. I don't remember what exam we had in the afternoon, but I remember after school, I had a quarrel with Hasan Lash about a "Book Jones" close-up shot. I hit him so hard in the chest with my head, that his head was thrown back against the school pine tree. Before I could run away, I saw that our math teacher had cut me off, almost at the door of the school. I wanted to pretend it hadn't happened and go on my way, but he reached me with two strides, and caught me by the scruff of my neck.

"So now you're a bully, you bastard, eh? Now I'll show you."

"You can eat whatever shit you want."

"Eh—you impudent bastard!"

He slapped me on my neck. I guess he hit me hard, since I was dizzy. I put my hand on my neck and closed my eyes. I shook my head a bit while my neck flushed hot and made my hand warm. Then the dizziness stopped. When I opened my eyes I saw the Usher beside him, hitting a switch against his trousers. The Usher didn't have any scores to settle with me, but the math teacher did, and that was enough. The worst thing was that the principal didn't come in the afternoons, or if he did, he left before the last bell rang. For a minute I considered spitting in the math teacher's face. Nothing could have made the situation worse. But I realized I couldn't do it in front of the Usher. He was very clean, and always smelt good, and he had forgotten my deceiving him about my short trousers. So I closed my eyes again, put my hand on my neck, and rested my left hand against the wall. There was nothing wrong with me, only that at first my head was dizzy. With my eyes closed, I heard them muttering, and next I heard the math teacher going away. Then the Usher asked, "Why did you hit Hasan?"

"He wanted to steal something, I didn't let him."

"What did he want to steal?"

There was no answer to this. Among us students, it was not done to talk about our private affairs with anyone. Especially things to do with films, which were absolutely forbidden. I stayed quiet.

"You should have come and told me!" the Usher said.

He spoke harshly. Not like at first when he was gentle. I still stayed silent.

"You're grown up now, boy. You must know you can't behave like this with teachers. I'll give you one hour's detention so you may correct yourself. And you should know that next time you will be expelled."

His voice was slowly getting louder, but all the boys had left. while my neck was stinging they had come one by one, and then slunk away behind the math teacher and the Usher.

So my mind was at ease.

Then the Usher, with fire and fury, called the Janitor and handed me over to him, saying, "Keep him for an hour. Ruin his Thursday night, then he'll learn to speak properly."

He handed the switch to him and left.

The Janitor, closing the door after the Usher, gave me the switch, and said, "Put it on the Usher's desk and come to class 2."

I rushed and put the switch down and went to classroom 2. The Janitor was struggling to lift the benches onto the desks so he could sweep the floor. I went to help him. I don't know how long it was before we'd put all the benches on top of the desks. When all the classes were ready to be swept, I said, "Shall I go and get some water to sprinkle about so you can sweep easily?"

He looked at me and said, "No, son, tomorrow's Friday, and it's getting late. I'm afraid your father Haj Aqa'll tell you off. Go and wash your hands while I lock up after you."

I ran towards the pool. I didn't tell him that my father had gone to Qom that morning. He knew my father, but he only came to the mosque on the nights of *Ahya* in Ramazan. I looked after him well whether I was serving myself or not. Tea after tea, thanksgiving sweets, dates and candies. And in fact he'd done me a service. We called him Mashdi Yahya. I suppose it was at last year's *Ahya*. I used to say *Aqameh* when my father led the prayers. When the service was over, he pulled me over to a corner by the door, and said, "Of

course Haj Aqa himself knows best, but it's a pity that you say
Aqameh. That's work for ordinary boys." And he started to leave.

I thought for a moment, then realized that he was right. So I ran
after him and asked, "By the way, Mashdi Yahya—what's the connection between your name and the nights of Ahya?"

He looked at me and said, "I wouldn't have been a janitor if I
knew about those things. Go and ask Haj Aqa." And off he went.
From then on, I didn't say *Azan* or *Aqameh,* and that's why my
father thought schools were responsible for irreligion in children.

I had washed my hands and face in the school pool, and I was
thinking like this and playing with the water, when I heard the sound
of the school door. I had forgotten where I was. I told myself to hurry
up, but when I wanted to stand up, I realized my feet had gone to
sleep. I rubbed my thighs a little. As I stood up, I felt the nape of my
neck still burning slightly. Coming out of the school gate, Mashdi
Yahya said, "Don't tangle with that fool. He's only just abandoned
his turban himself, and he's got no patience for the clergy. Give my
regards to your father."

IV

It was sunset when I got home. The door was shut. That meant
my father had gone somewhere again. My youngest sister opened
the door. I pinched her cheek, saying, "You idiot, why are you so
late?"

"Oh God, mother, it is bloody 'Abbas again!" she said.

How quiet the house was. It was always like this at sunset—you
could tell from the doors and the walls that my father went to the
mosque at that time of day. But on this occasion he hadn't gone to
the mosque. He'd gone to Qom. When he was in the house, you
could tell he was there even when he wasn't ordering people about,
had nobody with him and there was no light on in his room. It was as
though the air was heavy. Everything was quiet and in its place.
Nothing could be touched. Dared I annoy my younger sister then!
But now he wasn't at home....I went straight to the kitchen.

"Hello, mother. What's for dinner....?"

I saw my mother's aunt, sitting down cleaning something big,
heavy and shapeless. Mind you I felt ashamed. My mother was sitting on her low stool by the stove. She didn't raise her head to

answer me. That meant she was crying. My mother's aunt stood up and put the big thing in the corner of the kitchen. By the wall. Then I caught the gleam of the lead. The small smokeless flames from the stove on the pitted uneven surface of the lead, as if each one flickered there. At once I remembered my sister. I ran upstairs. In the twilight of the sunset, my sister was stretched out with a blanket covering her up to her chin. Her eyes were closed. Her husband was sitting by her, holding his head in his hands. His back was shaking. At the sound of my steps, he looked up. I saw his face was wet. He shook his head slowly, and in reply to me said, "Abbas dear, they're taking your sister from us...." and he sobbed, like the crying of old men by the pulpit. I couldn't stand it.

I rushed downstairs. "Mother, what have you done to my sister? How does Sanambar know and I don't?...."

Perhaps I was crying again—I don't remember. I say this because of my mother's aunt's reaction to me.

She put her hand on my head, saying, "You should be ashamed of yourself, son. You're grown up now. A man shouldn't speak to his mother like that."

She took my hand and led me out of the kitchen, whispering to me that I should go to their house and bring I don't know what. It sounded as though she said "shoud" or "shrout"—whatever it was, I didn't understand. Their house was beyond Paqapuq. I was surprised. I didn't know how I could get there and back in time. But there was no choice. I went straight there. The whole way I thought of the spider, cancer and my sister and that "dey put 'ot yead...." At my mother's aunt's house instead of giving me something and sending me back, they kept me there, gave me supper and made me sleep. The next morning my mother's cousin took me to Shah 'Abdol'azim, and when we went back together to our house, it was still quiet and empty, and there was nobody at home except my younger sister and one of the older ones. While they made tea for my mother's cousin I went upstairs. There was no sign of my sister, nor her bed. But the same spider was still sitting in the corner of the window with its web and small balls of flies corpses, as if nothing had happened. I was so angry that I took off my shoe and threw it at it. I threw it so hard that I broke the top glass.

Translation by A. Reza Navabpour and Robert Wells
University of Durham

3

THE PILGRIMAGE

"Ziyarat" [The Pilgrimage] was Al-e Ahmad's first published short story, appearing in the March 1945 issue of the literary magazine *Sokhan*. A year later, it was reprinted in Al-e Ahmad's first collection of short stories called *Did-o Bazdid* [Exchange of Visits]. "Goldan-e Chini" [The China Flowerpot] and "Eftar-e Bimowqe'" [The Untimely Breaking of the Fast] (selections 4 and 5, below) are also from *Exchange of Visits*.

The translation of *"The Pilgrimage"* here is an expanded revision of the partial translation by Henry D.G. Law that appeared in *Life and Letters* 63, no. 148 (December 1949), the first anthology of English translations from modernist Persian literature. The story itself is presumably autobiographical and describes events of part of the same trip depicted for other purposes in "al-Gomarak va al-Makus" [Customs and Excise], a translation of which appears in *Literature and Society in Iran — Iranian Studies* 15 (1982). In the latter story, Iranian antipathy toward Arabs is depicted. But, in "The Pilgrimage" the focus is almost exclusively on the narrator's personal feelings in the midst of a most important traditional Shi'i Moslem experience, the pilgrimage to the shrine of the Shi'i third *imam* Hosayn at Karbala, Iraq, near where Hosayn and his followers were killed in 680 in their unsuccessful attempt to wrest the caliphate from the Sunni caliph Yazid.

I

Three times I passed beneath the Koran, the water and the flour, and the third time I kissed the Koran and laid it against my forehead. My relatives, breathing out their prayers and holy phrases, filled the air with an odor of mosque and sanctuary—a sanctuary from which only the smell of burning fat and the sharp tang of tallow candles were missing. Then amid the tears which streamed from the eyes of my two sisters and my younger brother I went out of the house. Everyone I met on my way to the street, whether friends, strangers, neighbors, or others, as soon as they realized that I was setting out on a pilgrimage, implored me from the depth of their hearts to pray for them. I could not avoid answering each one of these believers with a salutation; at the very least I had to repeat to all of them the formula: 'I too need your prayers.' Some of them who were among my closest friends would not let go of me till they had whispered the call to prayer in my ears or quoted appropriate texts from the Koran to escort me on my way.

What was I to do? I could not, at this very last moment, break the hearts of these faithful servants of God. I could not fail them. Nor indeed would it have been pleasing to God that I should be a cause of distress to others. So I had to take this little trouble, vain though it might be.

How many people kissed me and prayed for me on my way to the street, how long the journey lasted I do not know. But I do know that as I placed my foot inside the droshky I heard the low sobbing of two or three old women from inside their long black chadors. These chadors were creased with age, and had obviously just emerged from the bundles they had been wrapped up in for years and years.

Till this day I had not understood that other men had the same sort of desires that I had, and I did not know that this longing I have in my heart is a sort of melancholy which visits everyone. Only now was I finding out how ardently these others wished that they could be in my place, could obtain their desire of going on pilgrimage to the Holy Places. This very day, as I was leaving my home, I heard someone who had discovered where I was headed utter a supplication to his God. The Arabic words came from the depth of his throat. "O God, grant unto us...pilgrimage."

I did not know whether to rejoice or to grieve. The customary flow, the tenuous current of my life, was now encountering a great shift with this pilgrimage. And this shift, willy nilly, was invading my brain, was invading my very existence, so quiet, so orderly, with the pounding and hubbub of a turbulent stream. I could not understand it.

I had no other thoughts as I went my way; and till the moment when I reached the garage, the moment when I had to give to all and sundry the little gratuities which custom prescribes for the intending pilgrim, I could think of nothing but the soup which would be prepared at home after I had gone—the soup with the long thin noodles which my sister would cut, the bowls full of mint with the marks of burning on them which would be sent to my relatives, and the party and the feast that would be held at home in honor of the occasion, and finally the prayers that would surely be said at the party for my safe return.

Well, that is Iran. And those are her customs: The vegetable pilaw with fish on New Year's Eve, the New Year's display of seven things that begin with the letter 's', the rice soup, the samanu, the noodle soup, and a thousand other things like them. Customs that at first sight seem silly, useless, trivial; but which in reality are created by and conform to the pattern of that special Iranian life...Oh Iran, Iran!

The kissing was finished. My pockets were empty of the small cash which I had been giving away. And though we were supposed to start about sunset, it was now three hours after nightfall. I had just eaten my evening meal standing up when the bus arrived in the middle of the prayers and felicitations of those who were there to bid us farewell. The bus was twisting its way through the dark and silent streets of the city. And under God's protection it was taking us away to the holiest of places on earth.

II

In front of the iron bumper of our steed, the main road was rushing towards us—even faster than we were travelling. It seemed to be terrified of us, for it sheered off on both sides and left the way open for our vehicle. Behind us too it fled away, as if frightened at our boldness. You'd think it knew we were all pilgrims.

Through a hole in the floor beneath my feet, I could see the fine hard sand on the surface of the road. It formed two parallel lines, broad and colorless, as if they marked the flight of an arrow speeding from the bow. On every side of the road things were flying from us. I wasn't clear whether they were frightened by our imposing appearance or whether they had not yet recognized who we were. Never mind. Let everyone, let everything fly from us. We were going to a place which all men yearn to see, for which they pour out their sighs and their tears. Though all men fled from us, that which we desired was flying to meet us: that holy city which appears to others only as a sweet vision in their dreams on dark nights, the city from which is opened a doorway to Paradise, which was going to let us enter through its sacred gates.

We had been on the road for days, and for more days we would be the guests of the desert and the empty spaces. Our monotonous life of the town had by now changed into another monotonous life—that of the desert.

On our way we had come across nothing except the little coffee shops which were sort of outposts of the towns near by, which in fact bore the same name. And in these coffee houses we had come face to face with an aspect of monotony which is typical of everything to be found in the vast desert that is called 'Iran'. A bench at the edge of the road, beside it the small smoke-begrimed door of the coffee shop. Inside, long broad benches underneath a domed ceiling. These benches were covered by dusty flat-woven rugs, or matting made of rice stalks from Rasht; and on these, in turn, were sitting bent, dried-up, preoccupied men, the air heavy with tobacco or opium smoke. Now and again in coffee houses which were near some town or village, we could see some bottles of wine in a corner or at the back of the room. And if we chanced to arrive late at night we were greeted by drunken cries or the snores of bus drivers dust stained and burnt black by the sun.

Everyday life passed in one particular environment tends to make us adapt to all the little details and pattern of that environment, and to cause the people we see every day to lose all significance sometimes. But these unexpected chance meetings, these cursory, transient glimpses of another life sharpen and clarify many truths we have not realized hitherto.

There was a coffee shop we stopped at one afternoon. Our driver had assured us that the owner was a true Moslem and a man of faith and piety. It had been arranged that we should have our evening meal there before we went on. The sun was still high in the sky, and the little coffee shop which faced west protected its travellers and customers from the heat of the summer sun with a home-made roof of matting and straw. Beneath it were sitting a group of men wearing felt caps on their heads, their knees drawn up under their arms. Unlike the country folk who frequent these places and talk of nothing but their cows and their donkeys, or who has just died, or of the parties they have been having for mourning or merriment, these men were silent, listening intently to a mullah who had just arrived from a nearby village in anticipation of the coming Moharram mourning days. He was chanting in a clear fresh voice a *rowzeh* on "The Departure of the Caravan of the Family of the Mantle." I had crept into a corner by myself, and was sitting on the edge of a bench listening to the mullah chanting. His voice went on and on. The sun's heat made me thirstier every second. That great red disc slowly descending in the sky seemed to me like the bloodstained banner of those two beloved sons of Fatemeh...

Soon I ceased to hear the mullah's voice. My mind left the place where it was, and I fell to thinking of the pilgrimage I was on, of the tomb awaiting us, of the tip I'd have to give the driver's helper, of the sermons I'd hear at the shrine, and of the pilgrimage prayers I'd recite, the sepulchre's cool silver grillwork I would be kissing, the bit of cloth I would attach to the doors and walls of the sepulchre as proof that I had prayed there. I thought of all these things and of many others...

A fellow traveller woke me up. It was nighttime.

The bus was racing along, and thanks to the presence of us pilgrims, and the prayers which were being offered up, we hadn't had one single flat tire so far. I heard the wife of a haji who was sitting beside her husband in the seat behind mine, say to him in the middle of one of his long discourses, "Do you see what the Lord has done? It is surely His power alone which has made this *hautobomile* understand that it is carrying us into His presence. May we be His sacrifice."

I had made friends with a middle-age man sitting beside me. He was a grocer by trade and he told me his story. He had a family of five to support and until two years ago was drawing a miserable wage from his master who had a shop in the Qazvin caravanserai. The day came when he could bear it no longer. One evening in the mosque he broke down in front of the entire congregation and prayed to God to deliver him from the dog's life he was living, before he became too old: to get him away somewhere where he could have a house of his own however small, set up a little shop of his own perhaps, and have enough left over from his own needs to spare a morsel of bread as alms for the poor. "There is no doubt whatever," he said, "that God took pity on me that night; for somehow or other in these last two years I have been enabled to escape from my drudgery. After goodness knows how many loans and borrowings I succeeded in laying out a little store of my own in that same Qazvin caravanserai, in a very small way of business, I admit; but I *was* my own master; and later on God willed that I should get out of that wretched bazaar. I was able to rent a tiny shop in Sirus Avenue. Now I have been able to save enough to go on this pilgrimage. My poor old father (God rest his soul and all those who have passed away) was very anxious that I should do this. "My dear boy," he said, "if ever the day comes when you can go into that Great Presence, do not forget me, do not forget me." He was my father. God has given him His mercy and forgiveness. And indeed, now that I *am* going, I shall remember his departed spirit, and I shall pray that from the darkness of the tomb his spirit may befriend him."

I was not the only one over whom my friend the grocer poured his favors. The other passengers, too, shared the warmth of his ceaseless flow of talk and of the stories he told to amuse us. Now and again he would start singing. He had a pleasant voice which I can well imagine used to delight men's hearts when he was a young man singing at mourning parties, caravan songs and such like. At night, when we were trying to close our eyes and snatch an hour's sleep in that cramped and uncomfortable camp-bed of ours, the pleasant chatter of Mohammad Hosayn went on and on inside the bus, went round and round in our brains...

I closed my eyes. I was exhausted. It was near the dawn. I felt a lovely cool breath of air coming in through the open windows on my face and neck. It stole through the open collar of my shirt. It crept round my chest like cold water. I was thinking of nothing. I am not even sure whether I was asleep or awake. But I heard someone singing in one of those groups, and the sound of the voice mingled with the noise of the engine..."Every...moment...to...my nostrils... comes...the fragrance of..."

I could not tell whether it was my friend singing one of his wonted caravan songs, or whether I was dreaming, or whether the morning breeze was bringing to my ears this familiar tune from some unfamiliar voice outside.

III

The entire space was filled with the hum of muffled voices. The heat, the pressure of the throng sharpened my thirst; and now my one desire was to get a drop of water down my parched throat. I pushed and forced a way for myself outside the swirl of men. Somehow or other I got my hand on to the sepulchre and pressed my burning face against the cool grill-work that enclosed it. I shut my eyes for a few minutes to recover myself.

I heard a woman beside me pouring out supplications and prayers that her wishes might be granted, in between the sobs which never seemed to give her any rest. From time to time she shook the strong framework of the sepulchre with her feeble hands; she only succeeded in moving the padlocks which are attached to its edges and corners. Some of the crowd had managed by force and with great difficulty to walk round the sanctuary. For all I know they may have vowed to themselves that they would kiss the whole of the trellis work. When they found that I refused to budge or give way to them, they lost heart. I suppose they put off the completion of their vow to some other quieter occasion. Anyhow they let me know very clearly by their whispered grunts how annoyed they were with me. But while I kept my eyes closed, I felt something gentle flow over my head and face from above. I knew very well how greatly all those others I had left behind me wished they were in my place, wished that they could pick up a little bit of the sacred dust and earth of the sepulchre to take back home as the most precious gift possible for the people of their town or village, to cure the sick and save them from knocking in vain on this door or on that...

IV

My thirst had now gone, and the heat of my face had changed to a pleasant coolness. My task was over. I had accomplished the pilgrimage. Once again I fixed my gaze on the tomb and the precious stone inside the trellis of the sepulchre, and once again the hidden desires in the core of my heart stirred and boiled, and came forth in a long-drawn sigh. I don't know exactly what it was I wanted, what my need was. Once more, I thought, just once more I'll close my eyes.

And now I had made the round of the sepulchre. The smell of cheap cigarettes, the breath of the thousands of pilgrims passing in and out of the crowd mingled with the smell of their perspiring bodies and filled the air with a peculiar and noxious odor, which was softened by the smoke from the twigs of aloes-wood, slowly burning in every corner. Words from the Koran echoed and re-echoed beneath the lofty domes. Those Arabic words poured out like rain and charged the whole place with holiness. On doors and walls, on the friezes, on the glasswork of the ceiling which reflected in countless broken fragments the images of that vast crowd, on the front and backs of Holy Books, on the prayer books in men's hands, on the threshhold of the sepulchre and all around it, on the great silver padlocks of the Shrine—everywhere those Arabic words were inscribed in thousands of designs and figures and scrolls, on wood and tile, on brick, on silver, on gold: everything was absorbed by their power. God knows how many years these words have been there, looking down upon all those who come and go, with importunity and with indifference.

For long, long years so many men in their great need have rubbed their faces against those figures and inscriptions when they could draw near them, have bathed them with their hot and bitter tears, that little by little they have lost their splendor. Nothing survives now save pieces of clean and polished silver or gold which conceal inside their hearts the hidden secrets of men throughout the centuries...

Everyone was in a special state, and no one there was a spectator except for me. One man was squatting in a corner and had twisted around his neck the end of the small turban he had put on for prayer. He had put his head against the wall and wept openly. And from a distance I can only see his lips moving and then once every so often turning upward toward his tearful eyes.

How fortunate these dead people are...I hope and pray that when I die people treat me the same way. Really and truly with this treatment a human being will never fear death again. The dead body is carried round the sepulchre: with the greatest veneration and dignity men carry it around several times and then leave. The odor of all the camphor with which the body had been sprinkled hung in the air, and plunged me into thought. I wondered sadly why the dead can no longer be buried in the sacred precincts themselves. But I will remember hearing from a preacher that the sanctuary environs extend for hundreds of square kilometers and that Nakir and Monkar would not dare enter within those boundaries. Although I am certain that when I die my body will not be able to rest inside the Sanctuary, even though I were to demand that in my last will and testament, still, at the least, I shall be laid in the cemetery nearby. Truly, then, I no longer fear death. Would that I could die now, at this moment, and...but no, I had forgotten. I haven't made my will yet and said where I want to be buried. Besides how mindless I've been not to get my burial shroud ready yet. Very well then, let me first go and buy myself some burial garments and carry them around the sepulchre myself, and then write a will and say where they should bury me, and then let me go and die in peace!

Translation by Henry D. G. Law

4

THE CHINA FLOWERPOT

"Goldan-e Chini" [The China Flowerpot] is the shortest story in the 1946 *Exchange of Visits* collection. The twelve stories in this collection—two others are "The Pilgrimage," selection 3 and "The Untimely Breaking of the Fast, selection 5 —portray a variety of Iranian social customs, character types, and conflicts, among them traditional Iranian New Year's visits, a Moslem funeral procession, sessions of religious sermons, the selling of votive candles at a mosque door, and goings on in a public women's bath.

The story set in a women's bath is called "Tajhiz-e Mellat" [The Mobilization of a Nation] and appears in David C. Champagne's translation in *Major Voices in Contemporary Persian Literature—Literature East and West* 20 (1976): 64-70. One of its themes is Iranian helplessness in the face of the Allied Occupation of Iran during World War II. There may be at least an echo of this theme in "The China Flowerpot" as well, when the owner of the flowerpot exclaims at one point, "We're a nation worth nothing." But the main thematic thrusts of the story as social commentary have to do with individual acceptance of responsibility for actions *vis-a-vis* the sense that many things are fated to be, and the question of the responses of onlookers to interaction conflicts they observe.

The bus filled up and started to move. The last person to board was carrying a valuable, antique, china flowerpot and, trying to maintain his balance, headed warily toward the rear of the bus. There, the people in the back seat jostled each other and somehow found room for the man with the china flowerpot. He was a man of forty or more, wearing a stylish overcoat and a smart, new hat. The hand that gripped the flowerpot was encased in a new leather glove.

There were four other passengers in the back seat: two women in full-length chador veils who were laughing almost hysterically at some private matter, and two other persons, one an old man, bent and preoccupied, and the other a devil-may-care sort wearing neither shirt collar nor necktie. His shirt sleeves, their cuff buttons long since come off, protruded beyond the cuffs of his stiff, starchy trenchcoat. His hair fell below and outside a beat-up hat. A grey, mottled beard covered his freckled face, right up to beneath his eyes.

From the moment the dapper one, flowerpot in hand, sat down next to this latter, he attracted the whole attention and thoughts of the latter, whose eyes riveted upon the flowerpot.

The owner of the flowerpot sat quietly. He set the flowerpot on his knee and held it by its base. With his ungloved hand, he jingled some small coins. But his neighbor, totally absorbed in scrutinizing the flowerpot, appeared agitated. He raised and lowered his head, tilted it this way and that, striving, however possible, to observe this delicate and beautiful flowerpot more closely. Perhaps for the first time in his life he was face to face with beauty; or if not, perhaps it was the first time he comprehended the meaning of beauty.

It was a fine china vase. On its two slender handles a design had been so artfully painted that the handles seemed to merge into the painted background of the body of the vase and could be distinguished only with difficulty. It was so fine and delicate that it transmitted the light coming through the bus window and gleaming on it, and cast a pulsating shadow on the leather glove of its owner's hand.

The fellow in the raincoat had by now viewed all the details of the side of the vase facing him; but he was not content with that. At every corner the bus negotiated, the passengers then lurching to the opposite side, he took advantage of the moment and slouched a bit more in the direction of the vase owner so that he might get a glimpse at that other side of the vase as well. He tried hard, but without much success. Finally, after priming himself a couple times and throwing out his chest, he spoke—the vase owner by now aware of his neighbor's discomfiture.

"Excuse me, sir. Would it be possible for me to take a look at your flowerpot?"

"Certainly, by all means. My pleasure. It's really nothing much." And presenting the vase two-handedly and somewhat cautiously to his dishevelled neighbor, he added, "But I beg you..."

The other cut him off abruptly and said, "Please rest assured. With the utmost caution. I won't be that long."

And he began inspecting the vase. From the front and the back. From beneath and above. He even scrutinized the vase's interior. In the meantime, the owner's eyes followed the latter's hands. And although the former tried to present an image of unconcern, while he kept his head facing forward and endeavored to read the brass, prayer-formula medallion tacked on the roof above the bus driver's head, from the corner of his eye he surveyed the vase and the movements of the hand of his neighbor, who, having inspected the whole vase, now held it up to the bus window. He put his hand in front of the vase and examined the pale red light that was reflected through the vase and around his fingers and the shadow of his own hand that slightly darkened the interior of the vase. By moving the vase forward and backward in relation to the bus window, he increased and diminished the colorful and detailed chiaroscuro effect...

...At another corner, the bus turned. And the passengers, caught unaware, jostled one another. He likewise lurched, tottered, and having no rail or grip by which to maintain his balance, unwittingly released his hand from the base of the vase and let it go...and the vase fell and, with a barely audible noise, broke into three pieces.

The bus hadn't yet fully negotiated the turn when the groan of the vase owner rose up.

"Oh, no!" And he said nothing else, but merely stared in bewilderment at the pieces of the vase.

His nonchalant neighbor bent over, and, while retrieving the vase pieces, said, "It's all right. Nothing really happened."

Thereupon, the vase owner, who had just returned to his senses, suddenly burst like a pomegranate and, colored with adrenalin, roared, "What else could happen that wouldn't be all right?"

"Nothing, *Aqa*. Listen. The vase just broke. That's all. It was just one of those things."

"What!? You bum. You've got some nerve."

"*Aqa*, maintain your dignity, please. Why say things that don't make sense?"

"You say it's nonsense. You son-of-a-bitch. If you hadn't seen the vase, would your cross-eyes have gone blind?"

At this point, the others realized what had happened. One of the women seated next to the men assumed a compassionate mien and said, "Oh, dear. What a beautiful vase it was. What a pity. But, *Aqa* is right. *C'est la vie.*"

The owner of the vase cut her off thusly, "Madam, what are you saying? I paid seventy-five *tomans* for that vase. You think that's nothing?"

The culprit added, "Okay. Granted. What's to be done about it? Give it to someone to put together again…"

The other woman spoke up from beneath her prayer shawl, "Fine, brother. But what happened? Are you all thumbs?" To which the culprit, while arguing with the vase owner and without turning his head toward the woman, replied, "Lady, no one told you to stick your nose in."

"Well, I never…God bless us. The owner's right, absolutely right. This guy has some nerve. He wants to bite my head off," she replied.

The vase owner had just bent over. Having removed his glove while holding the vase pieces in his hand he shouted, "I thought I was being neighborly. We're a nation worth nothing. And now that the vase is broken, he says it was fate. He thinks I'm going to let him go. Well, I'm going to collect the last penny of the price of the vase. You'd think money was hay. I buy a vase, You break it. Then you say, 'Have it fixed.' You spastic. What's an antique to you? You haven't even the brains to look at one. Of course, I'm a fool for treating a lummox like him with kindness."

And, as the bus reached a station, he added, "*Aqa*. Stop the bus. The police station's near here. Let me exercise my duty toward this man…" And, standing up, he turned toward the driver and said, "*Aqa*, don't let him get off till I bring a policeman and have all the passengers attest to what happened…"

And before he reached the door, he turned, standing in the center of the bus, and repeated his request to all the passengers and proceeded to get off, once more persuading the driver not to drive away.

Some of the passengers discussed the incident among themselves. A couple of people merely watched and laughed. The two women were still giggling, but no one paid them any attention.

The culprit talked to himself, "Okay. What can be done? It's not that I did it on purpose. So it fell and broke…"

The driver's assistant was hawking for customers.

The vase owner had gone some twenty paces from the bus. The bus driver, who had spent a couple minutes motionless and sunk in thought, stirred, straightened himself behind the wheel, called to his assistant, put his foot on the accelerator and took off...

The passengers were dumbstruck, their mouths hung open. And the driver's assistant, in answer to these mute protests, spoke up from his stool, "Okay. what business was it of ours? Someone else has broken a vase. Are we supposed to stay put and do nothing?"

The vase owner was hurrying toward the police station. He suddenly sensed what was happening. He turned and raised his hands as if to prevent the bus from leaving. But the bus merely swerved a bit and went on.

"Stop...stop them...vase...the poor driver...hey, officer," he cried out.

Seeing his state, the passengers began to laugh. Policemen now surrounded the vase owner and were inquiring what happened. But he merely cried out, "Stop them...seventy-five *tomans*...the lummox...a china flowerpot...they've gone...what was the license number...officer!"

Translation by the editor

5

THE UNTIMELY BREAKING
OF THE FAST

"Eftar-e Bimowqe'" [The Untimely Breaking of the Fast] is another story from the 1946 *Exchange of Visits* collection. Also, like "The Pilgrimage" (selection 3) and "Seh'tar" (selection 6), this story has to do with religious customs and attitudes, specifically the duty of a practicing Moslem to observe a fast from dawn to dusk during Ramazan, the 9th month in the lunar Moslem calendar. "The Untimely Breaking of the Fast" is a typical Al-e Ahmad story in its criticism of how Shi'i Moslem institutions, regulations, and customs can unduly influence those Iranians without the intelligence or judgment to think independently about their religious lives. Translator Carter Bryant discusses this story in "The Transformation and Rejection of Religious Values in Modern Persian Fiction," *Twentieth Century Persian Fiction: Critical Essays* (1983), wherein contrasting attitudes toward religion termed Nietschean and Marxist are distinguished. The Nietschean view involves a total rejection of a religion's institutions and moral order; whereas the Marxist view rejects institutions but not the presumed nobility of the ideals and morality behind them. Al-e Ahmad, as an individual ultimately convinced of the relevance of Shi'i Islam to his own life and its social significance in Iranian identity, would thus fit into this so-called Marxist mold. He strongly criticizes the hypocrisy, superstition, deceit, and ignorance that he finds in Shi'i religious institutions and practices, but he does not reject the value of religious faith.

I

Amiz Reza lay on the roof of his house on his bed-mat, fan in hand, covered to the waist by an old blanket.

The warm wind which blew across the sun-baked adobe rooftops of South Tehran brought with it the noise of the city's crowded streets or the protacted wail of a bus-horn or the far-away, sleepy, soothing melody of a musical instrument from a radio in the home of some well-to-do family. The wind played across Amiz Reza's sweat-soaked shirt but failed to alleviate the warmth of the early evening air so as to cool him off, lying there, his shirt pulled up over his belly, fanning himself with a raggedy old fan.

The dust which normally obscures the early evening Tehran sky still rippled above the dust-choked area of South Tehran. And the faint gleam of a street lamp and the outline of its pole and wires could barely be made out through the thick, mute, clouded air. Had it not been for the formless radio antennae and the wooden poles which held the mosquito netting in place around the neighboring rooftops, the eye would have beheld a solid canvas of seemingly endless adobe. As far as the eye could see, one could make out the edges of the rooftops, of roof trusses, high and low, even the outline of a wind tower dispensing clammy underground air into the dusty, suffocating atmosphere of the area.

The walls surrounding the rooftops, high in places, low in others, afforded one a view of everything going on around him. Now, in the dim light from the street lamp and the mute, colorless light of the new moon could be seen the mats and bedding freshly laid out on the neighboring rooftops, straw mats, or old, torn curtains upon which were placed thin mattresses and old comforters with worn spots where the cotton stuffing showed through. The rooftops were still empty. The neighbors had laid out their bedding for the night and left until the heat of the sun deserted the rooftops and eventually enabled them to consign their weary heads and battered bodies to sleep and achieve a moment of peace.

The clamor uptown had still not ceased nor the blare of the autohorns faded away. The voices of two newspaper vendors, loud and clear and wailing, carried a summary of the day's news from out of the midst of all the noise and confusion of uptown to the ears of the people in South Tehran, who neither have literacy to read a newspaper, nor, even if they did, the wherewithal to buy one.

The cries of the beggars in the streets were gradually dying down. They who from morning had spread their wares in niches and corners of a thousand shapes and sizes, the more pitiable the better, intimidating passers-by with those wares of poverty and misery, made good use of the darkness of the alleyways, withdrawing one by one from the field of their endeavor into the dark back alleys, an air almost of success about them, dragging along behind them their sighs and their moans and their gratuitous prayers and blessings.

It was the eve of the seventh day of the blessed month of Ramazan. Amiz Reza, who, at the evening hour of the breaking of the fast had eaten as much as he could of watermelon and drained cup after cup of ice water, had come up to the roof before the others to lie down and fan his swollen belly.

He was wondering silently to himself how he would ever possibly be able to observe the fast this year without cheating some on his fasting and his prayers. The blessed month of Ramazan had only been on for six days, and he, who, out of prudence, had begun fasting seven days ago, was already going out of his mind.

The hunger wasn't so bad for him, but the thirst! God in Heaven, the thirst! He who was no more than a minor bazaar broker and had to dash around from here to there, all day, every day, from sun-up to sunset, under this hot sun, how could he allay his thirst?

He was not one of those prosperous brokers at the heart of the bazaar who were able to secure several years' income with a single transaction and were thus able to crawl into a cool corner of the columned hall at the *Jame'* Mosque and spend the hours from ten to three there praying, then head straight for the cool cellars of their houses to emerge only just in time for the breaking of the fast. Nor was he a merchant with a reputable, established firm, to drive comfortably to the bazaar in his own car to check on his business a little before noon, then return to Shemiran and loll about on his well-cushioned lawn furniture in a cool corner of his garden, his sweet little newly contracted bride beside him. Nor was he one of those godless atheists who seized any excuse to get out of observing the fast.

Amiz Reza was a broker without capital or fortune, and he was a religious man who had never been content, like some of his compatriots during these last few tumultuous years, to wheel and deal and secure his fortune. Thus it was still necessary for him, in order to secure bread and water for his wife and children, to do a lot of scampering here and there around the bazaar.

He had managed up to now to get one daughter married off, but his new son of barely five months had managed to turn the brightest day into darkest night for him and for his wife recently, due to the heat and her lack of milk; especially these first few days of the blessed month, with his wife unwilling to break her fast, the child brayed continually, making life just that much more uncomfortable for his parents, his little testicles swollen from all that bawling.

Amiz Reza was content to wind up deals for four bales of sugar and a couple of loads of turmeric in a day and did not strive to do much more than this, feeling that any effort beyond this would serve only to wear out his slippers needlessly. It was almost as if he knew that on the day of creation it had been recorded and ordained that his daily lot should be even less than this. Whenever he managed to net more than this or managed to pick up on one or two extra deals during a month, he would become dismayed and incredulous, certain that he was taking bread out of the mouths of others. And so that these rightful profits of another might not stick in his throat, he would, if it were winter, make a pilgrimage to Qom, if it were summer, to Farahzad or Evin, to stay for a few days with his wife and children and pay homage to Emamzadeh Davud.

It had never even crossed his mind to desire a pilgrimage to Karbala or Mecca, and whenever he saw other people in a mosque or anywhere else sighing and moaning for God to grant their desires, he would sink into his own thoughts. He would lay aside whatever verse he was reciting or reading and stare, stupefied, at his prayer-stone. At such times he could never understand the thoughts that were going through his mind, but he was certain that he had never had such lofty desires and had never uttered even the humblest prayer in their behalf.

With his blind-man's literacy he was able, whenever his older son brought a newspaper home, to read the name of the newspaper and the titles of the articles, but not to understand the articles themselves, and he would ask his son to explain them to him.

One thing really bothered him, and that was that his son, who had finished sixth grade the year before, did not know how to read the Koran. Even worse was the fact that whenever he went to the school to complain about it, they would answer him in a totally insolent manner, "My dear Sir! Why press the issue? Do you think it will do him any good at all in his future life? Who even bothers with such things these days?" He was unable to reconcile himself to these vague and evasive replies and would constantly heap curses upon the system, or, rather, upon his wife, on whom, in his helplessness, he would focus all the blame.

During the day, as he walked through the streets of Tehran, he never had the time to ponder why people had, of late, become more godless than they had been in years gone by. But he could never tolerate seeing some brazen atheist eating something or smoking a cigarette in the street during the blessed month of Ramazan.

Walking along reciting a prayer to himself, he would think, "God, be my refuge! These days it is hard to find a man who does not stand among the ranks of the unbelievers!" Perhaps they wished to express their hostility to the dear month by smoking cigarettes in the middle of the street, and, if not, then they must make such display of themselves only to anger him.

He found it hard to believe that godlessness had become so common and that people would boast so openly of it, lacking all concern for and all fear of and all shame in the face of God and His faithful servants. Up to now a couple of times he had confronted these oafs and riddled them with curses as unrestrained as the blessed month of Ramazan would allow. One time it had even ended up with his having to pay a five-*toman* and two-*rial* fine, and if the police chief, may his father rest in peace, had not been a good Moslem, it would certainly have cost him a lot more. They might have sued for damages or thrown him for a while into prison.

He had told his wife absolutely nothing about that particular episode that had occurred on the second day of this Ramazan, and no one else knew anything about his smacking that miserable beggar, who had been sitting by the road smoking a pipe, smacking him so hard that he had bloodied his nose for him.

The beggar that day had certainly learned his miserable, leeching trade well, for he had raised such a ruckus and had protested his innocence as an ignorant stranger to the city so loudly that people had soon gathered round saying to Amiz Reza, "My good man! He may be ill. God will not condone your striking him."

Amiz Reza had answered them, the veins of his neck bulging, face as red as flame, "May his foul neck be broken! Let him crawl into some broken down hovel and slobber over any snake venom he wants in private! Doing it out in public like this is a declaration of war on God!" Then a policeman had appeared upon the scene and led him off to the police station to be fined. Even with all that there was still something to be thankful for, and that was that it had not ended more expensively for him. In spite of all this, to tell the truth, deep within his heart, he was pleased with himself for having struck a blow against the evildoers of this world.

But tonight, because he was so tired, Amiz Reza could not manage somehow to get to sleep. He was still lying there, fanning himself, wondering how he was ever going to make it through the vigils of those special, blessed nights of Ramazan this year, with him in this shape, his belly swollen from all the water and watermelon he had gorged simply to quench his thirst at the evening breaking of the fast, and beyond the vigils, how he was ever going to make it to the mosque the following morning to perform his duties there.

These last six nights it had taken all his strength to drag himself up to the rooftop. Trekking all that way to the mosque, reciting extra prayers in penitence for the prayers he had missed already, staying up all night until dawn, making it through the *Kamel* and *Samat* and *Jowshan-e Kabir* recitations at least three times each night, and at the end of it all placing the Koran upon his head to call, *"Ya Allah w'al-ghows*—O God and help,"...he had indeed reached the end of his rope.

The fast could not be broken. But if he were to observe the fast, every night it would be the same lot, and how could he, who every night, following the breaking of the fast, could do nothing but lie there limp and lanquid as a corpse, dare neglect his duties on these blessed nights?

He thought to himself, "Out of an entire year there are only these two or three nights. Everything would be accomplished, everything ordained, on these two or three nights; forgiveness and mercy—distribution of our daily portions—the meting out of our destinies, all of these would be translated from the mind of God onto those imperishable tablets which decree our fates. And should he fail to take advantage of this year's opportunity to make up for all his past ills, who knows, he might be suddenly struck down and die and never live to see another Ramazan. In that event, what disgrace, what dust and ashes would be heaped upon his head!"

Amiz Reza thought so much that he finally drifted off to sleep.

II

It was two in the afternoon. The street-front stores were all closed and their owners were surreptitiously lunching behind closed doors, or, if they were of the faithful, they had already gone to the mosque to hear the sermon.

The bazaar had ceased its racket. Those with nothing to do took refuge from the hot sun of the streets under the shade of the domed arches of the bazaar, worn completely out by the heat. The shopowners fanned away the flies, having given their errand boys and clerks a break to spend talking over among themselves the tips they'd got so far that day or the goods belonging to their various employers that they had been able to sell on the sly, getting each others' opinion and advice.

Amiz Reza, who, in spite of all his running around that morning, had still not managed to close even one deal, someone having managed to snatch two loads of turmeric, which he had been promised for a spice merchant client of his, right out of his grasp, virtually stealing it from him at one *shahi* less per *toman*, came, dizzy and despondent, out of the mosque.

He had no idea, in this condition, how he would ever manage to perform his prayers. He had not read the section of the Koran required of him every day and had not even waited for the preacher, who had been a little late today. He had rolled up his prayer mat and taken his slippers from the foot of one of the pillars of the mosque and stuck them under his arm, taking his *tasbih* beads in hand so that he could perform at least his post-prayer recitation on the way, and had left the mosque.

He wasn't sure just how much distance he had covered that morning, but however much it had been, his tongue had grown as dry as dust, and his brain was nearly exploding from the thirst. However much he thought about the plains of Karbala and the thirst of Zahra's children, he was still thirsty. However much water he poured over his head from the pool in the courtyard of the mosque with the little brass cup he carried in his pocket, it had given him no relief. He was going mad.

He emerged from the courtyard of the mosque. But where to? He himself could not have told you. Today he left the bazaar behind much later than he did on other days and found himself out beneath the burning afternoon sun. He was not consciously heading for anywhere in particular, but where was he heading? Perhaps in the back of his mind he knew where he was going but did not wish this subconscious knowledge to be revealed to his conscious mind and was making an effort not to take it into account.

He took his skull cap out of his pocket and placed it on his head. He put his *tasbih* beads which he had up to now forgotten to count and recite back into his pocket and quickened his steps. He boarded the Number 2 bus and went straight to the Qazvin bus station.

He could hardly remember ever having been on a bus or in a taxi, but he was after all from Tehran and knew how to find his way around the city. Besides, his thirst was driving him into a frenzy.

The bus for Karaj was full up and about to pull out when Amiz Reza caught it. He sank down onto his seat among the other passengers in the right rear corner of the bus. The bus made a fast trip of it, no flats or stopping to pour water into the radiator on the way. Nobody paid any attention to what he was doing during the trip. Only the bus-driver's helper noticed him and the fact that he was asleep while he was collecting his fares, and not having the heart to wake him up, let collection of this particular fare go until it was time for the passengers to get off. That very night, Amiz Reza himself, after the breaking of the fast during which he had botched it and told his wife about the episode, once he had squelched the argument that arose because of it, no matter how hard he tried to remember, could not have said how he ever managed to get himself to Karaj sitting in that rear corner of the bus, whether he had really fallen asleep or had fallen into some kind of a trance. The bus reached Karaj in an hour. The passengers disembarked and went on their own way. Amiz Reza, who up to then had never really familiarized himself with any part of the country around Tehran other than Shah 'Abdol'azim and Shemiran, managed to get himself to a coffee house by asking here and there. He pushed open the one leaf of the double door and entered. One or two hours later, when the departure time of the bus he had come on came round, he re-boarded and got to Tehran in time for the evening breaking of the fast.

III

At the time of the breaking of the fast that evening he neither ate watermelon nor showed any inclination to drink any ice water. He ate a few chunks of bread and some meatballs and downed a couple of teas on top of that. His wife, much too clever to let something like this go by unnoticed, seemed to have caught more than a trace of a whiff of what had happened. Amiz Reza, who was in no mood to try to conceal it, told her all about it.

His son burst out laughing. But his mother had only to snap sharply at him once to send him crying into a corner. The issue was hardly even worth discussing. But his wife—who knew whether she was upset over some fight she'd had earlier over a prayer mat in the mosque or whether she had simply borne a great deal of suffering herself over her own hunger that day—simply wouldn't leave it alone. She opened her mouth and out streamed a multitude of curses.

"Bah! You idiot jackass! I suppose you don't consider me a human being sitting in this damned house all day waiting for you to come home, my belly aching as if someone was twisting a knife in it! Don't you feel any shame to have spent four *tomans* to go all the way to Karaj just to drink a glass of tea and break your fast in the bargain! And in the afternoon at that, when you could have waited only two or three more hours! How can you hope for God's mercy now? You're not even man enough to keep His fast! Who said you had to fast anyway! You might have taken that filthy four *tomans* of yours and bought a bunch of grapes for your children to choke upon at the breaking of the fast!"

Amiz Reza, who really didn't want a ruckus to get started and feared lest the neighbors come to the edge of their rooftops and hear about the whole thing, tried to quiet her down and said to her in a calm, hoarse voice, "*Za'ifeh!* Enough! This kind of behavior cannot be pleasing to God. They'll hear you up there on the rooftops. What are you saying, woman? I know my duties better than you do. I asked the *Aqa* about the matter, and he said there was no problem at all. So why do you persist in…"

When she heard him say that he had asked the *Aqa* about the matter, she burst involuntarily into laughter, forgetting her anger, laughing uncontrollably, and said to him in a mocking tone, "Bah! May dust and ashes be heaped upon your head! For shame! You and your *Aqa*! A man who still doesn't know what his duties are!"

Amiz Reza did not wish to believe this last comment. However, somehow or other he managed finally to get her to shut up, and, in order to get everything quiet as quickly as possible, he took his fan in hand and went up to the rooftop.

His nursing infant son brayed continuously. The warm wind, which was still blowing across the rooftops, brought with itself the intermittent, far away, synchronous cries of mourners in who knows what corner of the city shouting their "Ya Hosayn! Ya Abolfazl!" to the monotone rhythm of men beating their chests. On a neighboring rooftop, in the weak glow of a kerosene lamp with a smoke clouded chimney sat a group of people listening attentively to one among them who was reading from a religious poem in deep, spirited tone.

The moon of the eve of the eighth day of Ramazan, nestling in a corner of the sky, stared upon the scene with a despondent, grief-stricken face and a pitying glance. A few of the stars in the sky, bereft of all their luminosity and strength from having gazed too long down upon all this ignorance and poverty, died all of a sudden, tumbling downward from their place in the sky into the world of darkness and terror, followed by a stream of light that consumed their last breath of life. Others, bolder and braver, like people who stare into the face of the sun, fixed their gaze straight down into the midst of all this misery and suffering and blinked for fear of going blind...or—Who knows? for I certainly do not—perhaps they had been overcome by laughter in the face of all this wretchedness and stupidity and were winking at each other in mockery of us.

Translation by Carter Bryant
The University of Texas at Austin

6

SEH'TAR

"Seh'tar" is the title story of Al-e Ahmad's third short story collection, which was published in January 1949. Several other stories from the *Seh'tar* collection are also available in translation, including "Bacheh-ye Mardom" [Some One Else's Child], translated by Theodore S. Gochenour in *Iranian Studies* 1 (1968): 155-162; and "Lak-e Surati" [Pink Nail Polish], translated by A. Reza Navabpour and Robert Wells in *Iranian Studies* 15 (1982).

A *seh'tar* is a small-bodied, stringed musical instrument with four strings that are plucked by a pick or the forefinger nail. The story itself is a classic Al-e Ahmad indictment of misguided Shi'i Moslem faith which, as a young man at the age of twenty-seven, he observed being practiced by many uneducated Iranians (see Preface, page xi).

He had in his hand a new, caseless *seh'tar* and was proceeding on his way with an open collar and carefree air. He hurried down the steps leading to the Shah Mosque and was making his way with difficulty through the middle of the stands of merchandise there and the people milling about looking for who-knows-what.

He held the *seh'tar* to his stomach and with his other hand took care so that the strings would not get caught on a button of someone's clothing or on the edge of something carried by a porter and break.

At long last, today he had been able to attain his great wish. No longer would he have to get a *seh'tar* from someone else when he wanted to play at a party, paying an arm and a leg to rent it and having to be grateful to others as well.

His hair was dishevelled and spilled over his forehead and covered his right eye. His cheeks were sunken and his complexion sallow. But he was ecstatic and strode along blissfully. If there were a party and the right situation arose, when he felt this way, he'd sing and play the *seh'tar* and affect everyone with his own inner and hidden joy. But now, among people who were milling about for who-knows-what reason, what could he do except hurry along and get someplace fast? He raced along out of joy and thought about the *seh'tar* that was now his very own.

He thought that from now on whenever the mood was upon him he'd get the pick acquainted with the *seh'tar's* strings, powerfully and without any conscious thought, he would no longer worry about the strings breaking and the *seh'tar's* owner turning his bright day into dark night. This thought made him feel good. He thought that from now on he would give such performances and get so much out of the *seh'tar* and produce such excitement out of it that he himself wouldn't be able to stand it and would suddenly start crying. He didn't know why he would break down and cry. But from the bottom of his heart he wished that he could play so well that he would break down and cry. He was sure that only when he cried had he played well. Until now he could not play as well as he wanted to. He had done all his playing for other people. For people who searched in the sound of his sad voice for joys that had been lost or that had fled.

All those evenings that he had sung and played at cheerful, joyous gatherings merely brought him an uneasy happiness. On all those evenings he had not been able to cry as a result of his own music.

He had not been able to play his instrument so that he could make himself cry. Either the gathering wasn't suitable or the people who invited him and paid him were unwilling to take in his tears, or he himself, out of fear of the strings being broken, would strum and pluck it a lot more gently than he could have. He was sure of it. He was sure that up to now he had played and sung much more gently and cautiously than he could have.

He didn't want there to be anxiety any more in his music. He didn't want to be cautious any more. Now that he had been able to buy an instrument with, as he put it, "unblessed" money, now he had fulfilled his dream. Now the instrument was all his own. Now he could play exactly what he wanted. Now he could play the seh'tar in such a way that he'd start crying.

He had been playing and singing for three years. He had dropped out of school on account of this. He always sat in the back of class and hummed to himself. Other students didn't take it seriously or didn't notice, but their math teacher was very strict. The humming bothered him so much that he would get angry and storm out of class. Three or four times he decreed that there be no humming in class. But how was that possible? Only in the last year did anyone not hear his humming in the back of the class. He was so tired and stayed up so many nights that he either stayed in bed till noon or slept in class. But this didn't last long either, and soon he dropped out of school.

The first year really wore him out. He sang and played every evening and every day slept till noon.

But afterwards he gradually got things organized and did not take jobs more than two or three times a week. Gradually he became known, and he didn't have to approach this or that musical group. People had gotten to know him and would leave instructions at his humble house with his mother, and they'd be certain that he would come and they would thus have a great time.

Despite all this, his work was still backbreaking. His mother sensed he was getting thinner day by day. He himself paid no mind to this. His only thoughts were of owning a seh'tar. And of being able to pay the seh'tar any way he wanted. But this was not easy to do. Only lately, on nights when a lavish wedding came his way, could he put something away and buy a new seh'tar. And now that he was the owner of a seh'tar, he really didn't know what other desires he had. Naturally one could have other desires as well. He hadn't yet given that any thought. For now he only thought about getting himself somewhere fast and giving his seh'tar a close inspection and really getting into it. Even on those occasions of counterfeit joy and merriment, when a seh'tar was in his hands and when he sang along with it, he would get into such a reverie and become so soothed that he didn't want ever to put the seh'tar down. But how was that possible? He was in other people's homes with the joys and pleasures of others. And he was only supposed to bring warmth to the gatherings of others. In all of these reveries he had never been able to warm himself. He had never been able to bring warmth to his own heart.

On long winter nights when he returned completely worn out from these sorts of parties and searched for the way to his house in the dark, he felt such a vibrant need for this inner warmth that he thought that without it perhaps he wouldn't be able to make it home. In such circumstances, on a number of occasions he had grown fearful. And, oh, how many nights in search of this warmth had he stayed till dawn in the corner of some tavern.

He was very weak. At first glance he seemed more like an opium addict. But the excitement that he felt today and the warmth that he was feeling from an hour ago, from the moment when he had become the *seh'tar*'s owner, had reddened his cheeks and caused his forehead to be hot.

With these thoughts he had reached the main entrance to the Shah Mosque and had stepped onto the smooth stone of its threshold when a perfume seller, who was looking over his shop next to the mosque door and fingering his *tasbih* beads in expectation of customers, suddenly jumped down from behind his stand and grabbed the musician's wrist.

"Atheist! with this instrument of infidels inside a mosque!? Inside the House of God!?"

The musician's train of thought was broken. The warmth that had so recently found its way to his heart vanished. At first he was somewhat confused, and then, gradually, he comprehended what the young guy was saying. To this point nobody had noticed. There wasn't much coming or going. All the activity was around the trinket sellers' stands. He didn't say a thing. He tried to free his wrist and continue on his way, but the young perfume seller wouldn't let go. He had seized his hand and hurled curses one after the other and made an uproar: "Godless wretch! Don't you have any shame before God? How shameless can you get?"

Once again he tried to get his wrist free and go on his own way, but the young guy wasn't ready to let it end so easily and apparently wanted to take out his own slack trade on the musician. Gradually, a few people noticed and gathered around them. But no one yet knew what it was all about. Nobody had yet gotten involved. The musician was really been held up.

It was obvious that something would happen soon. But the chill that had seized his heart again subsided. He felt a warmth in his heart and then in his brain. He became incensed. He lost control of himself and with his other hand gave the guy a hard smack on the cheek. The boy's breath stopped short and he swallowed his own curses and swearing. For a moment he was dizzy. He had forgotten the musician's wrist and rubbed his face with both hands. But all at once he came to his senses and sprang forward. As the musician was entering 'he mosque with his *seh'tar*, the perfume seller grabbed his coat and once again seized his wrist.

A fight started. A lot of people got involved. The boy kept yelling, cursing, calling the musician an atheist, boiling mad from the insult to the House of God, calling on all Moslems for help.

Nobody understood how it happened. He himself didn't understand either. Only when his *seh'tar* with its wooden body fell to the ground and crashed with a short and reverberating sound and split into three pieces, the strings all tangled and twisted, he jumped aside and stood dumbfounded and looked at the people. The perfume seller, certain that he had righteously carried out his religious duty, calmed down.

He uttered a heartfelt thanks and once again went behind his stand, smoothed his hair, and *tasbih* beads in hand, began reciting *zekr* prayers.

Like the strings of his *seh'tar*, all of the musician's thoughts were twisted and tangled. And, in the depths of a chill that returned to his heart and was gradually spreading to his mind, he froze and fell bent over into a corner. The cup of his hope, just like the body of his new *seh'tar*, had shattered into three pieces, and the pieces seemed to be cutting into his heart.

Translation by Terence Odlin,
The University of Texas at Austin

7

THE SIN

Also from the 1949 *Seh'tar* collection, "Gonah" [The Sin] is one of the number of Al-e Ahmad stories whose protagonists are Iranian females. Another is "Pink Nail Polish," cited in the introductory note to "Seh'tar." Then there is the title story of the 1952 collection called *The Unwanted Woman*, which is translated as selection 8. Another Al-e Ahmad story told by an Iranian woman is "Showhar-e Amrika'i" [The American Husband], which is included in the posthumously published *Five Stories* collection.

In "The American Husband," the protagonist describes her marriage to an American and life in Washington which ended in divorce when she discovered her husband was an undertaker. Al-e Ahmad was especially sensitive to American involvement in Iran. For example, according to *Ferdowsi* magazine, no. 829 (11 Mehr 1967): 8, he once turned down an invitation to lecture to a literature group at the Iran-American Society in Tehran merely because the organization was American.

Inspiration for "The Sin," which takes place on the evening of a *rowzeh* or sermon gathering where generally the deaths of Shi'i imams 'Ali and Hosayn are commemorated, may have come from experiences in Al-e Ahmad's own family life, because his brother Shams (oddin) described the fascination of one of their sisters with the fresh, cool roof-top bedding on summer evenings in a story from his *Gahvareh* [Cradle] (1975) collection.

It was the night of our weekly *rowzeh*. And I had watered down and swept the roof and laid out the bedding. It was dark, and the faithful of the *rowzeh* had come. We had surrounded the courtyard, which was now full of people, with long narrow carpets and arranged flowerpots at the sides of the small pool. Having finished my chores, I sat in the shadows at the edge of the roof and watched the courtyard. This was my custom in summers when we hosted the *rowzeh*. And that night also I watched the courtyard. I was sitting with my head and body in the dark so as to watch the courtyard below where the men were arriving one by one and sitting in the places they always sat. I remember well. There was the old man who seemed to laugh whenever he cried. He sat in his usual place on the floor next to the preacher's chair. My sister and I always laughed at the old man's crying, making my mother so mad that she would bite the back of her hand and make us ask for forgiveness. And there was another man who never covered his face when he cried. Nor did he lower his head like all the others who acted as if they were ashamed to see the tears of someone else. But he neither lowered his head nor covered his face while the preacher recited. He faced forward while the tears rolled down his face with its short cropped mottled beard. At the moment the *rowzeh* ended, he went to the pool and splashed water on his face. Then, still dripping wet, he drank some tea and left. I had no idea what went on in winter when the *rowzeh* was held indoors. But in summers these same things happened while I watched from the edge of the roof. I found the old man's personality appealing to me. And when I was alone I never laughed at his crying. But, whenever my mischievous sister was there, she'd burst out laughing and I couldn't help but laugh too. And then my mother would become angry. The other man had no predetermined place, sitting somewhere different each night. I was especially pleased that his crying was silent. And that his shoulders didn't tremble. He sat calmly, unflinchingly, and the tears rolled down his face onto his mottled beard. And I could see the tears and the dampness of his beard from the roof-top. That night he, like the others, had come and gone. He was sitting on a straw mat on the opposite side of the courtyard facing my direction. We didn't have enough rugs to place all around the courtyard, and so laid out reed mats at one end. The back of the courtyard was full, as usual, while those who were friends of my father sat inside the hall. The servant who carried the water on nights of the *rowzeh* stood in the shadows behind the flower pots and recited. I could only hear him because he prayed too loudly. I wanted so to pray loudly. What a strange desire! I remember well. From the time I had memorized my prayers this desire had lodged in my heart, but I never thought to satisfy it. I never satisfied it. Where can such a desire surface for a girl, for a woman, who mustn't ever pray loudly?

As I was saying, I watched the courtyard until my father arrived from the mosque and then quickly I moved away from the edge of the roof and stood up. It wasn't necessary to watch any longer in order to see what would happen, to see what the men would do. I didn't see my father when he arrived, but I heard the sound of his shoes as he walked from the *kucheh* onto the stones of the hall, and afterwards the flip-flop of his slippers as they hit the hall floor. I knew my father had arrived. And immediately I could hear the footsteps of several other pairs of shoes on the brick floor. These were the assistants in my father's mosque and the other disciples who returned with him. I knew further that my father would place his shoes in the corner of the wall, and would stand on his small Torkaman carpet a few minutes; and all the people sitting around the garden, and in the room, drinking tea, smoking water pipes, would stand in respect to him and afterwards take their seats all at once. I didn't need to see this. I knew it all. It was the end of the summer, perhaps in the third summer that on nights of the *rowzeh,* after laying out the bedding, I began going to the edge of the roof and watching the courtyard. My mother sneaked upon me a few times. I was busy watching and she climbed up the stairs, came up behind me, and called softly. Afraid and embarrassed, I darted away. Then I stood quietly in front of my mother and promised not to go to the roof edge again. As if I could keep from it! Is it possible for a girl of twelve or thirteen, as I was that night, to heed such promises? Anyway, I moved away from my place when my father arrived and I went over towards the bedding. I'm glad my father still didn't know that I was sitting at the edge and watching the men on *rowzeh* nights. It would be bad for me if he knew. I was sure my mother wouldn't tell on me. What a kind mother she was! She never, never gave us away but would always take our side and argue over the purchase of new *chadors* for us.

I remember well. The beds were spread. The weather was cool in the evening and I went over to my bed, though it was not mine alone because I shared it with my seven-year-old sister, and sat down. I saw that it was very cold. I remember well! No one ever forgets what one has desired greatly. But sometimes one also remembers the little things. I remember everything from that night. I even recall not paying any attention to a neighbor's daughter who had come up on her roof to spread the bedding and yelled over to me. I pretended to sleep and didn't answer. I don't know why I did this but my mattress was cold and I didn't want to move. After the girl went downstairs, I stood up and sat down on my bed. I don't know what I was thinking about, but an idea occurred to me. I felt that sometimes I desired to walk slowly over to my father's bed and lie down. I still didn't have the daring to imagine sleeping on his bed. I only wanted to lie down on it. My father's bed was the only one we laid out on the side of the roof. I, my mother, and the children slept on this side; and the bedding of my brother, two years older than I, was placed on that side at the end of our row. And I realized that I was ashamed of myself. But I couldn't help looking at my father's bed. Then I remember looking at the sky. And two falling stars. But it didn't happen. I stood up and slowly, slowly, crouching so that my head would not be illuminated by the light from the courtyard, I went over to the side of my father's bed and stood. His was the only bed with a sheet. I remember well. Whenever I'd make his bed, I would first shake the mattress, put a pillow at the top and fold a blanket at the foot, and smooth a white sheet over it all. The white sheet of his bed was so striking in the darkness that it stirred my thoughts and desires. A momentary passion. I would lie down only half an hour. Because it was an especially bright night, the fourteenth of the lunar month, the sheet glowed so as to resemble snow. The passion annoyed me. But until that night I hadn't dared do it. I don't know what it was. There was no one to see me. And if someone were looking, I don't know what they could have seen wrong in it. But whenever this desire came over me, I would become uncomfortable. My face became hot, my lips burned, and I was covered with sweat and nearly fainted. I would waiver a little and quickly get myself together and run toward our beds and fall on my mattress. I remember crying one night and then laughing at myself for doing so. I didn't even tell my sister. But how ridiculously funny my crying had been that night on my bed, between waking and sleeping, and my sister came up to tell me that dinner was getting cold. And that was the night the desire came over me and the symptoms and the discomfort were the same. I dreamed of the whiteness of my father's bed every night. But had I the courage to go near it? I don't know how I found the courage that night. Standing at the foot of the bed, staring at the whiteness of the sheet and the length of the mattress and later I couldn't understand how it was that for a moment I lost control of myself and fell upon my father's bed. The sheet was cold, cold, and it froze my back to the soles of my feet. It amuses me when I think of it now. Perhaps my coldness was from fear. But my face was hot and my heart beat quickly, frightened that I might be seen behaving in such a forbidden way. Like the time I was combing my hair when my father came in. I was so frightened, ashamed, terrified that I fled. And I am still embarrassed about some things. But my shame didn't last long. My back warmed again, the sweating stopped, and my face was no longer hot. And I went to sleep just so, reclining on my father's bed. My brother was attending school, and I was the only one helping my mother with the work around the house, and I was tired after a day's work and having spread the beds. But I don't know at all how I fell into an immoral sleep that night. Whenever I think about it, I still perspire with shame, and the hair on my body stands on end. Again, I don't understand what happened. I only woke up once and saw that my father's quilt had been pulled up over my chest, and it seemed that someone was sleeping next to me. Oh, you can't imagine my feelings! Oh, God!

I kept trying to change my position, slowly then quickly, wanting to lie on my side. I soon quit moving around, incapable of moving any longer, and remained still. I was wet from head to foot with perspiration. My body was feverish, my teeth chattered. I slowly moved my feet from under my father's quilt and brought my legs up to my chest. He was lying on his side with his back towards me. His hand was under his head, and he was drawing on his pipe. Since I couldn't turn over on my side, I could see the smoke from his pipe rising above his head. The *rowzeh* lamps had been turned off in the courtyard. There was no sound. The only audible noise was the distant clang of a tin bowl falling on a neighbor's roof. How soundly I had been sleeping. How did I fall asleep? My chin was still shivering, and I didn't know what to do. Should I get up? How could I do it? Go ahead and sleep? But how could I sleep like this next to my father? I wanted to demolish the roof and fall with its crash. Truly, what a sen-

sation! In these forty years of my life I have never had such a feeling
again. It was a frightening feeling. For a moment I wanted to cease
existing so that when my father regained consciousness he wouldn't
see me on his bed. I wanted to dissolve into the air like the smoke
that rose from his pipe. I didn't want my father to see me this
shamelessly lying on his bed. Such a feeling. Little by little the wind
was hitting my sweaty blouse and chilling me. But did I have the
courage to move?

I stayed still, unmoving, lying neither on my back nor my side. I
held myself in one position. I kept my legs against my chest and my
father still had his back to me and was stretched out and smoke rose
from his pipe. Sometimes when I think of that night, I wonder what I
would have done if my father finally hadn't spoken. I didn't have the
strength to do anything, cold until morning, frozen in place from the
fear and the shame. But finally my father spoke from under his pipe
and between his teeth, "Have you said your prayers, daughter?" I
hadn't said my prayers. But if I had said my prayers, I would have
lied and said I hadn't. But in the end, this was the way I could
escape, and free myself. I had lost partial control of my senses, being
so dissolved in fear and shame that at first I didn't understand what I
had said when I answered my father. Then I thought and
remembered. It seemed that I answered him, "Yes, I've said my
prayers." But as it turned out, this question and answer provided me
with the means to get up, pick up my shoes and run downstairs in the
instant of an eye blink. My father's question provided the opportunity
for me to set myself free. I went downstairs. When I came onto the
porch, mother noticed the pallor of my face and, frightened, asked,
"Why are you so pale?" And when I told her, I remember well, she
turned her head away quickly, and leaving the veranda, said, "Well,
daughter, you committed no great sin." But I continued thinking
about it until after dinner and my prayers were said. I was still embarrassed for myself and my behavior. It seemed I had sinned. It seemed my father's bed was a strange man who could see me. I realized
the problem was paradoxical. I believe now that the terror and the
embarrassment I felt was the shame of a woman who sleeps with a
man not lawfully married to her. All this having passed, I returned
again to the roof and slowly crawled onto my bed and pulled the quilt
up to my ears. I remember my mother sitting next to my father and
saying, "You mean you knew nothing of your dauther's fear? She
thinks she has done something terribly wrong." And my father

neither smiled nor said anything. The long draws he was taking on his pipe were the only sound, and I fell asleep.

Translation by Raymond Cowart,
The University of Texas at Austin

8

THE UNWANTED WOMAN

This is the title story of Al-e Ahmad's fourth collection of short stories called *Zan-e Ziyadi* [The Unwanted Woman] (1952, expanded edition 1964). It is the story of a woman's rejection by her husband and of different sorts of poverty in urban Iran. A similar story of rejection and poverty is "Someone Else's Child," cited in the introductory note to "Seh'tar."

In a commentary on "Someone Else's Child" in *Anduh-e Bipayan va Chand Dastan-e Digar* [Endless Sorrow and Several Other Stories] (1977), fiction writer and critic Feraydoon Tonokaboni observes:

> Feelings and emotions and kindness, for these people who must constantly think about their daily bread, are decorations and nothing more. And, to be sure, the person who suffers to the marrow of his or her bones from poverty hardly thinks about such adornments. And society has bestowed this poverty on these people. Not just material poverty, but cultural poverty and emotional poverty as well. The prime culprit: a misguided and misleading society, a society that was askew from its first brick.

How could I stay in my father's house any longer? In that house you'd think the walls were pressing on my heart. It happened just the day before yesterday, but these two nights I couldn't stand it even for a minute in that house. Do you imagine that I was able to sleep? No, not at all. I tossed and turned in my bed till morning. Wasn't it the bed I had always slept in? No, not at all, it was just like a grave. I was at my wit's end. I brooded and agonized till morning. A thousand evil thoughts streamed through my head. A thousand evil thoughts. The bed was the same one I had slept in for years. The house was the same: every day I had cooked in its kitchen; every spring I had planted tulips in its flower beds; I had washed so many dishes in its pool that I knew when the drain got plugged and when the faucet leaked. Nothing had changed, but I was suffocating. It seemed everything had changed for me. These two days not one glass of water has touched my lips. My poor mother, if she doesn't have a heart attack from worrying about me she has done something. Yesterday my father got up and went to Qom again. Everytime something bad happens he goes to Qom. My brother was so upset that he didn't say a word, not to me, not to his wife, not to mother.

How is it possible for someone not to realize that her very existence is the cause of so much suffering? How is it possible for someone not to feel that she is unwanted? How was it possible for me not to know? I couldn't take it any longer. This morning, after they had their tea and my brother left, I put on my *chador* and left too.

I didn't know where I wanted to go. I just headed down the *kuchehs*, fleeing those two days of hell. I didn't know what I wanted to do. I passed my aunt's house. I saw Sayyed Esma'il in the *kucheh*. But I had no desire to go in, not my aunt's house and not Sayyed Esma'il's. What good would it have done?

I soon came to the bazaar. The hustle and bustle brought me around and I began to think. No matter how much I thought, I knew I couldn't go back to my father's house again. After this humiliation! After this disgrace! After I had eaten his bread and lived in his house for thirty-four years! I walked along thinking; why does a person go crazy; why does she throw herself in a river, or eat opium? God forbid that that day come. But you don't know what happened to me last night and the night before.

I was suffocating. Both nights I went out to the yard ten times. I went up on the roof ten times. God knows how I cried, but I didn't feel better. Even crying didn't make me feel better. Who can one tell these things to? If she doesn't tell someone her heart will burst. How could this be endured that, after staying in father's house for thirty-four years, within forty days I was taken back and tied to his beard again. Now that everyone is talking about it, why shouldn't I? O God, you know it wasn't my fault. How am I to blame? I didn't ask him to buy me so much as one pair of stockings without good cause. He knew everything. He knew how old I was. He had even seen my face once. Father had told him it was lawful to see me once. He also knew about my hair.

Besides that, he wasn't exactly Prince Charming himself. He was a lame, ugly man with a scraggly beard and thick metal framed glasses resting on his big nose. O God, even if you forgive him, I won't. After all, I hadn't promised to sacrifice my life for him; besides, he knew about everything. Then why did he bring this calamity down on me? Why did he shame me? O God, don't forgive him. The damned bastard had come to see my father four times and had gotten in over his head. God damn him. It was all his fault. He had heard my brother describe me at the office. He did everything else himself. On Fridays he came to see father and he bowed and scraped until it was agreed that on the next Friday he would come to see me. O God, you are my witness.

Even now when I think of that day my body trembles. I remember as he came up the steps, I heard the sound of his lame leg and cane on the bricks and my heart almost leaped from my breast. You don't know how I felt. He came in and went straight to my brother's room, which was also the sitting room. My brother was with him for several minutes; then he called me to bring in the drinks and left on the pretext of getting cigarettes. I had made some *sharbat*. I put on my *chador*, placed the drinks on a tray and went out. The room I shared with mother was next to the sitting room. Mother tried to comfort me. She saw how pale I was. By the time I reached the sitting room door, it seemed that half my life had passed. It wasn't more than four steps, but it took a lifetime. Father wasn't home, my brother had gone downstairs to his wife to get cigarettes, and mother was standing in the doorway saying softly, "Go on dear, go on, God be with you." But my feet wouldn't move.

By the time I reached the door my endurance was spent. The tray had shaken so much in my hands that half the drinks had spilled. I didn't know what to do. Should I go back and fix the drinks or take them in as they were? The roots of my hair had perspired, and my body had turned to ice. My heart was ready to leap from my breast.

God, if he hadn't called me what would I have done? I was standing there unable to move when the bastard called out, "*Khanom*, if you're embarrassed, may I come out to you?" O God, you're my witness. Then I heard him dragging his lame leg across the carpet. He opened the door, took me by the wrist, and gently pulled me inside. When I think of that moment, my wrist still burns as if he had put a bracelet of fire on it. He pulled me in, took the tray and set it on the table. He seated me in a chair and sat down facing me. I thought maybe he would take my *chador* off too. But no, he wasn't that rude. God, don't forgive him. My *chador* was still on and, as I was sitting down, I pulled it tighter around me, but my face and neck were still visible. My face was burning and I don't know what state I was in when he began speaking. "*Khanom*, God himself has approved." Then he stood up, walked around my chair and sat down again.

I knew what he was doing. I flushed and didn't know what to say. I had to say something so he wouldn't think I was mute. No matter how much I thought nothing came to mind. How is it possible for a girl like me, who for thirty-four years in her father's house hasn't seen anyone except her brother and has hidden her face from all other men, who hasn't even talked to strange women except in the public bath and bazaar, to face a strange man and not lose her head. I wasn't one of those modern gypsies who has gone to school and known a thousand strange men. And a strange man had come courting, at that. I was struck dumb. No matter how I chided myself I didn't have anything to say. But suddenly God Himself came to my rescue. As I sat there with my eyes riveted to the table, I thought about the drinks. I suddenly blurted out, "Your *sharbat* will be warm, *Aqa.*" But I didn't say *Aqa* right, the word stuck in my throat, and I left it half finished. As his hand moved toward the glass of *sharbat*, I found more courage and said, "*Aqa*, would you like a cigarette?" And I flew from the room.

What a state I was in! If my brother hadn't been home and I had been forced to take him cigarettes...? But, God protect him, what a fine brother he is. What would I have done without him? When he saw how panic-stricken I was as I came down the stairs, he said, "What's the matter, Sis? What happened? Doesn't everyone get married?" He went upstairs with the cigarettes and that was the end of it.

That was the first time we saw each other. God knows that while

I was in the room somehow I wanted him to find out that I wear a wig. But I couldn't speak. I almost died just saying one word. Later, when I calmed down, I told Mother. She said, "It's nothing dear. Your brother will fix everything." I knew that if we didn't explain it right away it wouldn't do any good; after we married he would certainly find out. Since he would find out eventually anyway, why not tell him now? I knew that if he found out later at home, inside of four days he would take care of me. But what's he done now? And tell me how I dreaded it. O God, if you forgive him too, I won't.

What had I done? What wool had I pulled over his eyes that he treated me this way? I was ready to wait a year and, during this time, do the house work for his mother and sister. But he wasn't. I knew that people were sitting around saying that so-and-so went back to her father's inside of forty days. If I had stayed in his house a year, that in itself would have been something. Don't think I had fallen in love with him. God no, not with that haggling bastard with his lame leg. But maybe I could have gotten pregnant and in a year the kid would have come. I would have been satisfied with anything as long as I wasn't eating my father's bread.

I was just tired. Thirty-four years of waking up in the same house every morning and going to sleep there at night. And what a house it was! They were empty years with nothing new. No one came to see us and we didn't visit anyone. No weddings, and, I shouldn't say this, but there wasn't even any mourning. Nothing happened at all. After my brother got a wife and began socializing, the only new thing in our house was the tumult on the nights when water was brought in. At least that was something, but it only happened once a month.

You don't know what I'm saying. I don't want to say my father's house was bad. No, poor father, but I was tired. What could be done? I was just tired. I wanted to have a house of my own. I wanted to be a housewife, but his mother and sister took care of his house. I would have been satisfied to do the housework for them all. He could have waited a year. But he didn't.

Now I know why he paid more than half of my dowry in cash. It was seven-hundred and fifty *tomans* in all, and he paid five-hundred in cash. We spent it all on things for the house, and my mother got started on my trousseau. He owed another two-hundred and fifty *tomans* and when he took me back to father's house he said he would pay it when my waiting period was over. Now I know what an ass I was. Do you think that we had words, or that we fought, or that I said something bad that caused him to bring this disaster down on my head? Far from it! During those forty days we didn't raise our voices once, not me and not that loathsome son-of-a-bitch.

From the very first, when I saw I had to live with my mother-in-law I was leery, you know. A person can sense some things. I saw that a quarrel might arise and, being helpless, I was very cautious. Believe me, to them I was like a bad penny. They wouldn't have treated a servant that way. I had lived in my father's house for thirty-four years with honor and respect, and now I had become the servant of my husband's mother and sister. But I had no complaints. I was still satisfied.

Our wedding was very brief. The signing of the contract and the ceremony were together. Earlier, my brother had taken the household things and my trousseau to his house and straightened up the rooms. What a house, the whole thing only had two rooms and they had filled one of them with my things. That night after dinner they joined our hands and sent us off. Oh, I don't want to think about that night. God forbid. Such a short period of bliss.

I just remember that after the contract was signed, he came to kiss my cheek and I looked at his face in the mirror as he whispered in my ear, "*Khanom*, I've ordered a beautiful wig for you." You don't know how this upset me. I certainly should have been happy. Happy that he knew about it and wasn't upset and still accepted me in spite of everything. But it was like being hit in the head with a mallet. I wanted to reach up and pluck out his bug-eyes from behind his glasses. The loathsome son-of-a-bitch; a person has only one wedding night, and that isn't the time to be reminded of one's misfortunes. O God, may he never see a good day. I couldn't eat a bite of dinner. If he hadn't said what he did as we were walking down the *kucheh*, there's no telling what might have happened. I didn't have the least bit of control over myself. But God came to his rescue, I mean He came to our rescue.

In the *kuchéh*, as we were going to his house he whispered in my ear, "I don't want my mother and sister to find out. You know why?" I had an involuntary desire to kiss him, but stopped myself. All the bitterness and jealousy which had been stored in my heart melted away. It seemed like with this one word his love found a place in my heart.

God take his life. Now I'm disgusted with myself for swallowing his bull like that. How happy I was. Yet it was at this very instant that I first sensed something wrong, but I supressed it. When one's husband is happy, how can she harbor bad thoughts? I didn't think anything about it. But, the very next day it started.

That evening I went to pay my respects to his mother. He had told me to reproach her for not coming to our wedding. After I kissed her hand, I made my little complaint, and my, my it didn't embarrass her at all to say right to my face and that of her newly wed son, "I have no desire to go to a wedding which was planned without me. Understand? And don't bring this girl to my room again." May she drop dead just as unexpectedly. From the very first night I didn't have a chance. The old bitch. But he was so kind and comforted me so that I forgot about it. Somehow the night passed. Somehow all the nights passed. The days were what mattered.

During the day I was alone with those two bitches while my husband worked in the office of a notary public. From morning till noon when he returned and all afternoon till he came home at sunset I was in hell. I didn't even go near their room. I did my work all alone and stayed inside as long as I could. I straightened up our two rooms, swept the court-yard and washed the dishes. He had forbidden me to set foot inside my own house, and, fool that I am, I had consented. But after I pleaded with him for a week, he agreed to go once every other Friday night and eat dinner there. Later we made it once a week. But during the day I still didn't dare set foot outside my house. I had no place to go except the now mandatory once a week trip to the public bath. He bought everything we needed in the mornings before going to work. He bought everything separately for his mother and sister. Until noon, my heart was happy in knowing that he wouldn't come in emptyhanded. In the evening when he came home he would stop briefly to say hello to his mother and sister and, sometimes if they were making tea, he would stay and drink a cup and then come to our room. The bad thing was that the house belonged to his mother. It was during the second week that they started making me do their dishes too. I acquiesced in this also and, if I heard a voice coming over the wall, I knew they were calling me. But how was it possible to stop their vicious tongues? While he was gone, they had a thousand complaints and criticisms. They would walk past my door and say sarcasticly that I wore a wig, or that I had a pocked face or that I was forty. As if their son was Prince Charming.

It was the wig that finally ruined everything. How was it possible to hide it from them? Fearing they would find out, I went to my old neighborhood bath house. But one day his mother went there and, pretending not to know me and acting as if she felt sorry for my husband because he'd married a sour old hag with a pocked face, she sounded out the masseuse. God damn that masseuse. You'd think she'd given her an extra five *rials*. She told her about my wig and made fun of me. God damn them. What had I done to them? How had my good-luck-turned-sour and the ugly husband who had become my lot straightened their lives? Why were they jealous? God knows what she said. The next day a worker at the bath house told me about it. She even mimicked the way I take my wig off, put it on my knee and wash and comb it. I certainly didn't go back to that bath house again, but I didn't say anything either. I left and never set foot in there again.

How is it possible to look these kinds of people in the face? In any case there was nothing to be done. They knew what they must not know. After that my days turned black. Two or three times when my husband came home from work he stayed in their room longer than usual and once he even stayed for dinner. Again I didn't say anything. What an ass I was. You'd think that I had sinned, that I was the guilty one, that I had lied to him about my wig. I didn't come out and say one word to him. Then they made us buy everything together and go eat lunch and dinner in their room. After that I didn't eat a bite. O God, what an ass I was! They caused me all this misery and I didn't say a word.

Why didn't I think? Why didn't I persuade my husband to move out? I was ready to live in a stable as long as we were alone. What a fool I was to sit with folded hands and take whatever they dished out. It was all my fault. I sat in my father's house for thirty-four years and all I learned was the way to the kitchen and bath house. Ach, why didn't I learn to read and write? I could have saved a little every month, and like Aunt Batul, I could have bought a sewing machine by installments and done my own sewing. Our neighbor's girls learned to knit socks and, within a year, bought their own knitting machine and made enough to live on. They even made their own trousseau and it finally took ten porters to carry them off. How my brother nagged at me trying to teach me to read and write. But I'm good-for-nothing. It was all my fault.

Now I know that thinking about all this for two days was what put those evil thoughts in my head. I sat in a corner of my father's house for thirty-four years and felt sorry for myself because I wear a wig, because I'm ugly and because I wasn't married. Are all women beautiful? Is there anything wrong with all the people who wear wigs? Am I the only one with a pocked face? It was all my fault. I just sat there and listened to all his mother and sister's abusive remarks. I let him go to them and listen to all their sarcastic and unfair remarks until his opinion of me changed. Once that had happened nothing could change it.

The last night, when he came in from his mother's room, he didn't change clothes but stood in the doorway and said, "Wouldn't you like to go to your father's house?" My heart stopped. We had gone to his house two days ago on Friday, and had eaten dinner there. I suddenly knew what was up. I just said, "Whatever you want," and sat quietly mending his sock. He asked again and I gave the same answer. Finally, he said, "Get up, let's go, dear. Let's go see how they are." Ass that I am, I allowed myself to hope that it wasn't what I thought.

I gathered up my stuff, put on my *chador,* and we left. On the way, neither one of us said anything. We hadn't eaten dinner. A pot was in the fireplace. We would have taken it to his mother's room to eat. But the pot was still there when we left. My heart was vexed beyond description. It was like I knew what he wanted to do to me. But once again I put it out of my head.

Our house wasn't far. When we arrived and I knocked on the door, I had exactly the same feeling I had the day I stood behind the sitting room door and he opened it, took me by the hand and pulled me inside. Maybe I felt even worse. I was trembling from head to toe. My brother came and opened the door. As soon as my eyes fell on him it seemed I forgot all the sorrows of the world. I forgot what was happening. My brother's face showed nothing as he said hello and we went in. We walked through the hall and into the courtyard. My sister-in-law was there and Mother had stuck her head out of an upstairs window to see who it was. He followed along behind.

When we reached the middle of the courtyard the bastard turned to everyone and said loudly, "This Fatemeh *Khanom* of yours, I am returning her to you. Don't let her come back again." By the time I could scream, "Why! I won't stay. I won't let you go like this," he, lame leg and all, had bounded through the hall and closed the door behind him. As I stood there screaming, "I won't stay. I won't let you go," the tears began running down my cheeks and wouldn't stop for anything.

My poor mother was quickly by my side. She took me upstairs, all the while asking what had happened. How could I tell her that nothing had happened? Not a fight, no angry words, nothing. I finally stopped crying, I said that I had fought with them and that I had sworn at them. All lies! How could I say that nothing had happened and that the miserable son-of-a-bitch, just as easily as he had married me, had brought me back to father's house and left. It was too late to do anything now. The miserable bastard was gone, and that was that.

The next day he went to my brother's office and told him that he had divorced me and that, when my waiting period was over, he would pay the rest of my dowry. He said to send someone to pick up all my things. You see? My mother knew that his mother and sister were the cause of everything. But how could I live in my father's house again? How could I? The two days I stayed there were exactly like being in prison. I wish I had been in prison. There, at least, one wouldn't feel wretched from seeing her mother and father and want to melt into the ground. She wouldn't be so embarrassed by the looks of her sister-in-law. The walls of our house, which were so familiar, seemed to confine me. The domed roofs seemed to imprison me. I couldn't even drink a glass of water or get a bite of food down. Poor Mother! If she doesn't have a heart attack from grief, she's done something. And my poor brother! He can't bring himself to go get my things, but there's nothing else he can do either. Ach, that clubfooted little bastard, he works in an office and knows the score. He's no longer wet behind the ears. How do I know that he hasn't caused a thousand other disasters just like this one? But no. No worthless S.O.B. is more worthless or unlucky than me. And talk about his mother and sister putting me down, they're going around to various houses courting for their son. But which S.O.B. is ready to put up with those two bitches, except me. Damn it, I sat there with folded hands and let them destroy the one chance of my life.

Translation by Leonard Bogle,
The University of Texas at Austin

9

A PRINCIPAL'S FIRST DAY AT SCHOOL

This selection is the second chapter of *Modir-e Madraseh* [The School Principal] (1958), Al-e Ahmad's most popular work of fiction and the first important novel in post-Mosaddeq Iran. It is a first person narrative account of events during a whole school year set in the mid-1950s at a recently established elementary school in a new Tehran neighborhood. The novel's obvious purpose is social criticism, and the title character may seem autobiographical in some respects. His is a persona Al-e Ahmad later used in *Nefrin-e Zamin* [The Cursing of the Land] (1968), a much longer novel that criticizes, among other things, the effects on Iranian village life caused by the programs of the Pahlavi White Revolution. Both *The School Principal* and *The Cursing of the Land* are discussed in "Al-e Ahmad's Fictional Legacy," *Iranian Studies* 9 (1976): 248-265. John K. Newton's translation of *The School Principal* (Chicago: Bibliotheca Islamica, 1943), which includes an introductory essay on the novel's significance, is out of print.

The text here of "A Principal's First Day at School" is the translation, slightly revised, that Karim Emami published in "Crisis in Education: *The School Principal*," which appeared in *Kayhan International* on October 19, 1964.

The assistant principal was a tall young man, who talked in a loud voice, gave orders with ease, received visitors, and had made a deal with the bigger boys who took care of things on their own. It was obvious he had no need for a nuisance of an overlord and could well manage the affairs of the school without a principal.

The fourth grade teacher was a very big man, twice the size of a full-grown person. He was the most conspicuous object in the school office. One of those men whom you take for a director-general when you see them on the street. He spoke formally and it was perhaps for this reason that he delivered a welcome speech on behalf of his colleagues...

"Next year we shall have," he said, "godwilling and under your shadow, secondary school classes as well."

It was evident that his physique was growing too big for the elementary school level. When he was making his speech I could only think of one question: how was it possible to develop such corpulence and to maintain such a neat appearance on a teacher's pay? I decided to shave regularly every morning and to make sure that my shirt collar was clean and the crease on my trousers sharp.

The teacher of the first grade was a slim, wiry type with a dark complexion, a few days' growth of beard on his face, and an evenly-clipped head; and his shirt buttoned all the way up. No tie. He resembled the scribes who sit on the steps in front of the Post Office. He even looked servile. He kept silent, and rightly so. One could guess that such a person had only the courage to open his mouth in the first grade and only about capital "A" and small "b" and such things as that.

The second grade teacher was short and pudgy and instead of speaking, screamed. He was cross-eyed. And on that first day I could not find out where and what he was looking at when he addressed some one. Each short scream of his was followed by a burst of laughter, his own. You could see at once that he was the teachers' clown and that during each recess he had to come and amuse his colleagues. Nothing could be done about that. But I only felt sorry for the students who had to restrain themselves at his classes.

The third grade teacher was tall and slender, with a clean-shaved bony face on top of a well-starched white collar. When he walked, one could not be sure that he would not twist his ankle and come tumbling down. But he moved about like a whirling top. He spoke haltingly. His chest could only supply air for three words at a time. His eyes shone with something more than intelligence. There was something unhealthy about that gleam which prompted me to

ask the assistant principal if he was tubercular. He had of course no
T.B. but he was from the provinces and lived alone and also studied
at the university.

The fifth and sixth grades were jointly run by two men. One of
the two taught Persian and religious lore and history and geography
and handicrafts and other such pastimes. He was a young fop with
brilliantined hair and tight trousers, a fancy handkerchief in his outside breast pocket and a wide yellow necktie held onto his chest by
the carcass of a big anchor. His hands constantly rose to guard his
hair and he looked at his own reflection in the window panes every
other minute.

The other man who taught arithmetic and the computation of
percentages and interests and the rest of the subjects was a dignified
solid young man who had the looks of a Mazandarani. He was self-
confident and the only one of the teachers who always had cigarettes
on him. It was clear that he was successful in class. In addition to
these, we also had a sports instructor whom I first met only two
weeks later. He was an Esfahani and one of those smart alecs. He
would not turn up even three days each week and yet thought he
was doing us a big favor.

These were the men with whom I had to get along and with
whose help I had to push the school along. Keeping an eye over two
hundred and thirty-five children and putting knowledge into their
heads and leading them over the first obstacle was no simple job. But
for someone like me, who had escaped from the cage of teaching,
any place could be a paradise and any job a relief. That is why I put
on my trappings and jumped right into their midst.

...I made warm and leisurely inquiries about their well-being
and then I offered them all cigarettes. All cooperativeness and sympathy! I was glad that I would have an opportunity to acquaint myself
with these new men and to inform myself of their private sorrows and
to enter their enclosed worlds...I inquired about their family and
occupations. The third grade teacher was the only one among them
who attended the university. The one with the anchor dangling from
his chest studied English in the evenings to go to America. Two of
them were married: The scribe of the first grade and the director-
general of the fourth.

There was no tea to be had, and during the fifteen minute
recesses the teachers assembled in the office simply to show one
another that once again they had returned safely from their classes,

and then to start all over again. And this would not do. The tradition had to be upheld. I took five *tomans* out of my pocket and placed it on the desk and it was agreed that tea things would be purchased and they themselves would organize their tea, and the cross-eyed teacher got the assignment.

Then the bell rang and the children lined up. The assistant principal hesitated for a moment outside the office door as if he had something to tell me, when the director-general came to his rescue. He himself knew that with his physique he could get into the act anywhere and for any problem. And he gave me to understand that a speech on my part to the assembled students would not be a bad idea. I agreed.

The assistant principal had put the matter to the children in two or three words when I arrived on the scene and they all applauded. All heads had been clipped short and some of the boys had white collars and most of them had *givehs* on their feet. The tattered garments of a dozen of them were two or three sizes too large. It was the case of the hyena inheriting from the bear, as the proverb goes.

A red-haired boy who was standing in the ranks of the third grade students tried to hide the ripped corner of his pocket. The sixth graders were whispering to each other and at the end of the line two or three first graders were getting at their running noses with their coat sleeves, when I suddenly appeared in front of them.

I had nothing to tell them. I only remember saying that the principal had wished to have one of them as his own child but now he did not know what to do with so many children. They laughted silently and someone in the middle of the back rows let out a loud guffaw and I suddenly thought of the need for a special language in dealing with the boys. And then I was full of misgivings that "No, it's not so easy after all!"

Earlier I had thought to myself that I would go there and be free from all the worries of discipline and administration, lock myself up in my office and do my own work. There would be the assistant principal or some one else to look after things and there would be an organization that would run without my interference. But now I was beginning to see that it would not be so easy. What if tomorrow one of them bashed someone else's head, or if one of them was run over by a car or fell down from the upstairs veranda. What would I do then?... I don't remember what else I told them. But I recall that when the bell rang and the students began to file towards their classrooms I was full of sweat. I walked back and forth on the veranda to give the teachers time to move out and then I went back into the office.

Now I was left alone with the assistant principal when something crept furtively in through the door. It was a man. He was the school janitor, with a peasant face, unshaved and with a short body. When he walked, he would space his legs well apart and keep his arms away from his sides. When he talked he panted, as if he had just finished a race. He came in and stood by the door. He was looking directly into my eyes. I inquired about his health too. After all he could also lift one corner of the load.

He had a wife and a child who needed a playmate, and all for a salary of ninety tomans a month. He had been given the storeroom next to the toilets. But he had not succeeded yet in collecting his monthly stipend of five *tomans* as a caretaker. And yet he had bought a pair of rugs on credit for three-hundred and fifty *tomans* with two-hundred *tomans* still outstanding. In one minute he told me all his troubles and when he was through with his list of requests, I sent him to get some tea.

The assistant principal said the janitor had been a peasant on the estate of the school owner and that he had been employed by the ministry at the owner's insistence and that one whole article of the contract for the transfer of the school-house to the Ministry concerned him. It was obvious that along with his wife and child he was a part of the school dowry. I had learned by experience that dowry maids who accompanied the bride often turned out to be troublesome creatures.

When I said this, the assistant principal burst out. "He is such an ingrate with too much cheek, and on many occasions he has refused to obey the teachers..." and so on. Then I turned to his own case.

He had finished the normal school just one year earlier. He had worked for one year at Karaj and Garmsar and this year he was here. His father had had two wives. Two sons by the first one who had both become knife-wielding toughs, and himself, the surviving child of the second marriage who had managed to get himself educated and become known as such in the neighborhood. He had to support his invalid mother. For many years now there had been no sign of his father, and worst of all the high cost of medical treatment...and they had rented a single room for fifty-five *tomans* a month and a salary of one-hundred and fifty *tomans* did not go far and that at best he could only hope to benefit from the technical allowance of the assistant principal's job after three years...then we got to our feet for an inspection of the classrooms.

The second grade was next to the office and there the children were struggling to add 754 to 261. Their teacher would aim with his crossed eye at the third bench and arrive over the first.

Then there was the assembly hall. It was empty and large, filled by two white rectangular columns. And at the end there were three or four broken-down desks and benches and the opposite wall was covered by picture of champions and fighting men and Negro athletes and Egyptian weightlifters. And the righthand wall was covered with a large map of Asia. And "Presented to the school of 'Ali-Mardan Hendi" worked in underneath in the fashion of a trademark. Done in a crude hand with the blue of the seas as pale as a deadman's saliva and with its Caspian Sea in the shape of the bent cypress motif of Persian art and the railroads all generously wide and all trans-Iranian and even passing through Kerman, and the Indonesian islands all lumped together and joined to Singapore and in the bottom each fragment done in a different color. A collection of all available colors like a patchwork quilt! And each finger-tip with its well-demarcated frontiers as a sign of nationhood and with an army and an emblem and coins and postage stamps and barked orders and arrests and each in the hands of an Emir or a Khan or a Sheikh who along with his family or tribe was leading it towards the highway of progress and prosperity!

I was reminded of the days when I was passing through this stage myself and had to draw maps. I realised how much things had been easier for us, the children of twenty-thirty years ago! Even when we did a map of the world we did not need more than two to three colors for all Asia and Africa and Australia. We used brown for England and half Asia and Africa and pink for France and the other half of the world and green or blue, I don't know which, for Holland and the other few, and now...

"What a lot of work to do for the children!" I said this last sentence aloud and the assistant principal asked, "How is that, sir?" and I said, "Oh, nothing" and asked what they had been doing with the hall and it became clear that nothing was being done. No films, no gatherings, no plays. It became only useful at examination times. And if you sniffed a bit you could detect in the air the smell of the children sweating it out during their written exams and you could feel the heat of their fever. It was exactly like a locked up room whose stove had been put out only the day before. Involuntarily my hand touched the wall, which was not warm and then the columns which were thick and heavy. And how well they shouldered the burden of education!

Then we went upstairs. There were five rooms in a row and a sunny veranda running all the way in front of them. Koranic words, resonant and perfectly enunciated, came out of the fourth grade window and rang out across the open land which stretched at the foot of the school and was beaten down by the sun which also intensified the glare of the landscape's occasional tin roofs. The call of Islam! And how reassuring for the residents who had not yet come to dig in these lands for foundations and wells! There were no mistakes, no undue stops, no unnecessary elisions. I was certain that the teacher had nothing to do with it. Such a recital had to be the product of attending solemn Koranic sessions in the evenings. The products of our schools lacked even this much polish. The future residents of the neighborhood should have no worries.

The third grade was next to the stairs. The students were ordered to their feet and the desks rattled. They were writing a dictation. The teacher was whirling round the class on his slender legs and dictating "Sa'di is a humble man prostrate!" I looked at one student's notebook. He was writing "humbel man pro straight". We passed on.

The fourth grade teacher was solidly seated and it was a surprise that the chair withstood his weight. One could not see which one of the students was reciting the Koran. If we went in, the students would no doubt get up and it would have been disrespectful. I stuck my head in through the window with an "excellent!" and we continued on our round.

The fifth graders had computation of interests and the blackboard was full of digits and the teacher did not pay much attention to us. We passed on and as soon as we opened the sixth grade door and the brilliantined fop's "fatherless motherless b..." hit us in the face. One student was flushed red. It was no doubt the lingering cosmetic effects of the invective. They were having Persian Reading. The teacher had put his hands in his pockets and expanded his chest.

"Mr. Principal," he complained, "they can't appreciate friendship. They need to be beaten down on the head. You can see with what sinceri...".

I cut him short just before the plosion of the T with "You are right. But forgive them this time for my sake. They don't look like a bad lot."

And we came out. After the sixth grade there was another room, long and narrow. Like all the other rooms it had a door and a window looking south and a big window looking north. This was no doubt my future office. With a desk and a closet, and both empty. It couldn't have been better. Quiet, sunny, remote. When the door was closed you could not even hear the Koranic phrases, let alone the noise of the children from the courtyard below. And if the teachers wanted to see me about something, they would be too tired to climb up all those stairs. I settled the matter and we went back downstairs.

There was a big shallow pool in the center of the courtyard, the only part of the building in which some consideration had been given to the size of the tiny tots. A volleyball net was strung up across the front part of the yard, torn at two or three places and mended by bits of wire, and surrounding the yard there was a high wall. Just like the great wall of China. A high barrier to stop any possible flight of education. And at the end of the yard the toilets and the janitor's room and then a storage room for coal and then a classroom. The first grade. And the teacher was extracting "am-are" from a student onto the blackboard.

We cast a glance at the toilets. When we walked in through the door two steps led down and then there was a passage ending at the opposite wall. And to the left there were five closets. All without doors or a ceiling. A partition separated them. One could see right through to the bottom of the latrines. And such a big hole that a cow could well fall through. Around the mouth of each latrine a pool of liquid, and the terror of the children from falling into the black pits materially visible all over the place. I looked at the assistant principal who was matching me stride for stride.

"This has become an awful bother for us," he explained. "We have written more than a hundred letters to the Construction Department, sir. They say government funds cannot be spent on someone else's property."

"And they are right," I replied, "The Ministry property can never be so dirty," and we laughed.

It had been enough. We came out. While we caught our breath in the yard I inquired about the financial state of the school, its budget and such things. Each room had been allowed fifteen rials a month for cleaning. For such things as brooms, mops and chalk. With the assembly hall passed off as two the total number had come to eleven. The stationery and the administrative books were issued by the Department of Education. They had also an allocation of twenty-five *tomans* a month for drinking water which they had not managed to collect yet.

The stoves had been wood-burners the year before but now had to be modified for coal. There was a fund of three *tomans* per stove allowed for installation expenses each year. The school had also a petty cash allowance of thirty *tomans* a month that, like the water allowance, remained uncollected, and now we were in the second month of the school year. The middle of November.

I made it clear to him that I was not in the mood to run after such trivialities and I told him in brief my reasons for becoming a principal and I told him also that I was ready to give him all my authority. "Just imagine that no principal has turned up yet." He could also keep the school seal. Of course I did not know him. But I had to have an assistant principal. And who was better than he who had run the school in the absence of a principal for two months and was also a graduate of the normal school and knew what education was all about, and similar other compliments. I had heard the principals hand-picked their own assistant principals in advance but I had neither anyone in mind nor did I have the time and patience to run after such a person.

We made our stands clear and then went back into the office and drank the tea that the janitor had made for us with his own things, until the bell was rung and again rung and I had a look at the students' files which were composed of two sheets of paper each, a copy of their identity card and their small-pox vaccination certificate and an occasional record sheet of their previous years. That was all. And from these two or three sheets I gathered that most of the children's fathers were farmers and gardeners and water bailiffs, and I left before the final bell. I had had too much for the first day.

Translation by Karim Emami,
Tehran

10

GENERAL CHARACTERISTICS OF CONTEMPORARY LITERATURE

The foregoing selections have presented aspects of Iranian society seen and represented through the eyes of Al-e Ahmad as a short story writer and novelist. In this selection, it is Al-e Ahmad as literary critic who presents views about literary aspects of that society.

"Chand Nokteh darbareh-ye Moshakhkhasat-e Kolli-ye Adabiyat-e Mo'aser" [Several Points Concerning General Characteristics of Contemporary Literature] is the text of a lecture Al-e Ahmad gave to college students in Abadan in 1961. He later included it in a collection of eighteen essays on art, literature and society called *Arzyabi-ye Shetabzadeh* [Hasty Assessment] (Tabriz: Ebn-e Sina, 1965; Tehran: Amir Kabir, 1978).

One should ask a critic to discuss contemporary Persian literature. And whatever I may be, I am not a critic. Even if I had wanted to intrude upon this realm and offer a critical opinion, there was no time for study during this short trip. Besides, the date for my talk was set only two days ago. However, because the seeds of literary criticism have not yet fully matured·[in Iran] and because the leading literature experts often remain silent on contemporary literature — they don't get closer than subjects of a hundred years ago, busy as they are in the excavation of ancient graves and fearing a threat to their bread and butter in the discussion of living contemporary literature — I agreed, owing to the force of this backwardness, to cry out from the depths. And this in itself isn't all that bad. It conveys a change of taste. When in our universities heads are broken over having a chair for contemporary literature and when our elders, as followers of an ancient custom, are exclusively into resurrecting the dead, then a humble, non-university person such as myself is nococcarily forced at a university gathering to deliberate on contemporary literature. And this is something that happens somehow or other. Each new literary work that appears — each poem, tale and short story — constitutes another store in the edifice of contemporary literature. And whether we like it or not, the essential judgment is made by the writers and poets themselves who proceed with their work heedless of the opinion of this person or that. The essential judge is one who can judge.

I don't think it is necessary here to explain what literature means. It is a matter both simple and complex that I hope you have covered in class or have touched upon in outside reading. But as a backdrop for today's talk, I want to define literature very simply as a confrontation with life's questions and problems, that is to say, the encounter of an individual human being with life. An individual who, besides eating, sleeping, anger and passions, has also other concerns. Therefore, the aim of my talk is to provide a general sketch of the contours of contemporary literature and to define its general characteristics. Which is to say, let us see what characteristics this literature has that distinguish it from other literatures aside from the facts that it is in the Persian language and talks of our familiar [Iranian] environment.

We know that in philosophy they used to reach or are reaching the essential meanings of life and its primary causes and effects. In this fashion, philosophy too is a confrontation with life's questions and problems, but with the magnitude of questions or the great questions. In this sense, literature confronts exactly the same problems or questions, but through their details by means of inductive reasoning. If philosophy involves a search for the discovery of life's issues through deductive generalizations, then literature too arrives at the same generalizations through the investigation of individual and anonymous instances. Therefore, literature is the other side of the philosophical coin. Or at least forms a way to it, or is a branch to it. In any case, a writer or poet's confrontation with life and its issues is his or her philosophy. So let us see what the essential characteristics of this philosophy are in the works of contemporary writers. This has been the most general and at the same time simplest sketch I dared on such short notice to come up with for my talk. You'll forgive me if I went on too long or if it seemed no more than drivel.

Now, before I get to my specific topic, permit me to say something about a recent teaching experience I had and to express the hope that my educational colleagues here have had a similar experience. What happened was that at the beginning of the academic year I was teaching in a post-secondary technical school in Tehran, and it is obvious what. During the first class, the encounter with the students was such that I felt that the college administrators there were of the opinion that a technical school and literature just don't mix. For this reason I spent three whole sessions trying to make the students understand that it is necessary for them to know literature, to read and understand. However they thought that because they were involved in science and technology they couldn't have anything more to do with literature. They even thought that the heavens had opened and their excellencies had descended to earth as a gift for us. Like mana from heaven for the Israelites. Of course they were unaware of the fact that in this country the best graduate of a completely technical college is assigned ultimately to repair Western goods, to use them and make them work. Building machines is not something technical graduates get to do. This situation you'll agree is no cause for boasting and airs. If you only knew how proud these technical students were!

After three sessions of arguing I thought these gentlemen had been convinced, so I began teaching. But every day there were new signs of restiveness and objections proceeding from the mistaken assumption of the first day, all indicating a rejection of literature or at least a refusal to give it a chance. I realized that they were stuffing their ears with cotton so as not to hear anything about literature. This was why I saw it was no use and gave up. I realized that the hesitation of these great minds committed to science and technology in accepting literature is itself a sympton of *gharbzadegi* [Weststruckness], which I've discussed in detail elsewhere [selection 13]. That is to say, being misled by the naive thought that the only thing necessary in these times for the consumers of machines, which is what we are, is to learn about the size of cylinders, the rise and fall of pistons, and valves. My intent here in referring to these matters is to be clear in my mind as to where I stand with my present audience. For this reason, I'd like to ask my esteemed audience: How many of you have read all the works of, for example, Mohammad 'Ali Jamalzadeh who is a prioneer in this field [five of approximately three hundred persons in the audience raised their hands at this point]. Of course you should bear in mind that I did not ask: How many of you have read 'Ali Mohammad Afghani's *Ahu Kanom's Husband* which, despite its defects, is the most recent literary event in our language and times

Well, you see that I'm right not to be very hopeful. It's apparent that the climate here is the same as in Tehran. In any event, may God come to the aid of my fellow educators in Iran.

Now let's proceed to our subject of discussion. The first characteristic that generally meets the eye in contemporary Persian literature, whether in poetry or in prose is factionalism of all sorts. Factionalism between the classical and the modern, the old and the young, among generations, among classes, between optimism and pessimism, and among conflicting inclinations and disparate views. In any case, the factions in Persian literature are clearly defined. It's also true that for some time now these factions have clashed in the world of politics, that is, everything about them has become blended together. But literature does not lie. Literature is a world of intimate sincerity. It inevitably involves frankness. Inevitably, each person can belong to one side only, and does not have more than one side. Presently in the spectrum of writers we have old men who have wielded their pens since the times of the Constitutional Movement and who try hard to proceed step by step in tune with developments in society. But their works can be compared only with 'difficulty to those of younger writers who have just taken hold of the pen and whose age is less than a third of the other group's. The temporal gap that exists between these two groups is not greater than forty or fifty years, but the gap that separates their writings is even greater than a century. Each of these two groups necessarily take different routes and have different styles and language and views. As an example, between the precursor Jamalzadeh and Bahram Sadeqi, who has recently appeared with a European-style *Kingdom of Heaven*, the gap in time is not any greater than that which I've mentioned. But their works (without me intending here any sort of comparison) are as far apart as the gap that exists betwen Thackeray and Spender in England or between Balzac and Camus in France. But notice I'm not implying that age difference causes the gaps in views and the disagreements in encounters. Because the same temporal gap exists betwen Nima Yushij and Mahmud Azad or, to a point, between Ahmad Shamlu and Mehdi Akhavan Sales. But these three or four people tread the same path in the world of poetry. Of course, not that they employ the same style. No, but their views lead, up to a point, to a single sort of mental construct.

Of course, this factionalism doesn't exist only between genera-tions. It also exists among different points of view, and also with respect to various issues. For example, an outspoken, feminine stance that we see in the poems of contemporary poetesses is still an issue under discussion. One group sides wholly with them, and another, including both male and female writers, avoids that subject. There is still one group of writers who oppose this feminine content with a vengeance, as if it were a hundred years ago or even earlier. And there are others who find this feminine outspokenness both out-dated and insipid.

This factionalism has also occured with respect to writers' duties, with respect to the message that they have and communicate. There are still people who, in the manner of the ancients, believe that prose is useful only as the medium of expression in literary research, biographical writing, and orientalist studies (which, most of the time, are only a caecum of colonialism). Our colleges of letters turn out only these goods, and more than a thousand a year. But then there are also some people who consider even the whole planet small as the realm of prose. In poetry as well, there are some people who still think that the creator of the universe has put tongues in their mouths or pens in their hands only for words of welcome and adieu, panegyric, celebration and commemoration. And there are other poets who have dried a drop of their own blood in their every word. Of course here and there among our writers we have those estimable worthies who write on both sides of the fence. But you know it's only possible to eat bread at today's prices in the world of politics. But these games can't make it in the literary world. The complaints of these people are groundless. Excuse me for talking in generalities. If I wanted to go into detail and constantly give examples, the point would be lost. At the very least it would be enough to accuse me of having an axe to grind.

Another characteristic of contemporary literature, that arises from this factionalism may be termed pessimism; and this pessimism is not peculiar to the young. Both 'Ali Akbar Dehkhoda and Nima Yushij were also pessimists. But most of those who belong in this category are people who do not have connections with the influential and who raise their voices from well depths concerning contemporary problems. Pessimism toward the established powers, toward dominant social institutions, and toward life under the protection of the powerful. The criticism of the existing situation in works that embody the coloring and sharp or rarified odor of politics derives from this pessimism. Or works which, in avoiding political candor, flee to the age of Daqyanus cloaked in methaphors, allusions, and allegory. Also deriving from this pessimism is the seeking of refuge in mysticism which itself is a sort of negative resistance arising from pessimism and an escape from and rejection of reality. Here too lies the inspiration for seeking refuge in the representation of the strange and preternatural (i.e., eccentrism). My point is the depiction of unusual people and conditions and events. From Sadeq Hedayat in *The Blind Owl* and "Three Drops of Blood" to Amir *Gol'ara's*, "Misfortune," which is a pamphlet kneaded together recently with the same ingredients. And it is this pessimism that finally leads to Forugh Farrokhzad's "Divine Rebellion" or Akhavan Sales's "The Ending of the *Shahnameh*."

Another characteristic of contemporary literature is humanism. The inevitable upshot of pessimism toward the powers that be is optimism toward those without power. The oppressed. That is, paying attention to the people. Perhaps for this reason the language of contemporary literature has moved a little toward religious *rowzeh* sermons. But the attention paid to the masses and to their language and local dialects and the language of the bazaar and the streets is also a manifestation of this humanism. These days a writer or poet cannot any longer even pretend that: Yes, I'm writing for my shadow [as Hedayat's protagonist declares in *The Blind Owl*]. The relative attention paid to literature, itself the result of a limited increase in literacy and education (in their elemental senses), has taken even this excuse away from us. And this humanism is the writers' reaction to this relative reader interest, and is gradually turning into a matter of faith for writers, taking the place of other sorts of faith. We have very few, and perhaps not any, poets or writers who are not humanists, in the broad, universal sense of the term, and no one to be a fiery patriot or a defender of the aristocracy. And this situation really has me concerned because in today's bazaar one needs every sort of merchandise. I who have no access to the aristocracy need to be able to discover from writers associated with the aristocracy what exactly is to be found there. It's a shame that on this score even 'Ali Dashti and Mohammad Hejazi have chosen silence. Although the characteristics of their prose meet the needs of the aristocracy for romanticism, breast beating, and elevated prose, as I see it, nobody dares to undertake the real task since it appears that the dominant classes have been ostracized from the literary arena. And, of course, this is a very appropriate warning. One can even assert that if the access of the masses to the political arena were as open as it has been in the realm of literature, our situation today would be much better than it is. When I say that the masses have access to the realm of literature, it doesn't mean either that literature has resorted to demagoguery or that it has surrendered its prerogatives to the people. I know that this can happen only in the realm of politics. If politics and the weekly magazines fill their pockets with the people's money and look for the most vulgar and popular words and things to say, then literature burnishes its own image with the desires of the people and with its literary whip strikes the back of mass heedlessness.

For this reason one can argue that another characteristic of contemporary literature is that it is acquiescent and undemanding with respect to the limits of the arena it commands, the market it has, its income and the appearance of its collections of stories and poems. We know that there are very few literate people and even fewer readers of books and that in order to find more readers one must turn to the magazines. That is, we must step outside of the arena of contentment. And it may be for this reason that you gentlemen have had such limited access to literary works. What is obvious is that a writer or poet who doesn't want to sell him or herself for the sake of a large readership still cannot earn a living from writing. Consequently, literature in our country still doesn't constitute an occupation, and is more an avocation, an avocation more serious than an occupation. That is to say, it's a professional commitment full of difficulties and perhaps without a future as well.

The days when a poet or writer sought refuge at some royal court are gone. But in its place an audience of the general public has not yet opened up for writers. The refuge of public protection has not yet completely opened its doors to contemporary literature. This in itself is sometimes cause for confusion in the minds of writers who see themselves and their works as shifting sands. But it's clear that after all the knocking at the door, from within the sound of footsteps has arisen. I've heard these footsteps, and I hope that things will no longer be as Mas'ud Farzad described: "Closed is this door, hearts must seek another. And if this isn't possible, one must bow one's head in sorrow."

But, in any case, until this sapling grows tall and bears fruit, it will need a lot of care. There are still writers who print only two hundred copies of their works, paid out of their own pockets, and who plant each copy like a seed in plowed soil. This current state of things likewise intensifies writers' modesty and contentment. Sadeq Hedayat was only an employee in the College of Fine Arts while alive. But when he died, in the college auditorium they raised their voices in his honor and resorted to cannibalism. Ironically, the College of Fine Arts is a place that deals only with non-verbal arts. Or arts that have mute languages and are amenable to interpretation and have more to do with line, form, and color, and not with words that are obtrusive and candid and need neither interpretations nor interpreters. This is why the powers that be not only give protection to this sort of art, but also an arena. On the other hand, the expressive language of poetry and prose is more insistent and obtrusive than what one can use as a silent, eye-filling decoration on the doors and walls. In my opinion, years and years are needed for contemporary literature to be officially recognized. A person who has eaten a cantaloupe thrown away by the aristocracy and the authorities must necessarily sit down to calm his shaky legs.

Another point to be made is that contemporary literature has been greatly influenced by the numerous translations that have been made in the past twenty years, from the point of view of enriching the language and broadening views and opening up hearts. If we realize that the majority of poets and writers have themselves translated western works, we will recognize the importance of this influence. For my own part, very often while reading some poem or prose piece I have discerned the traces of some foreigner and his or her book on it. This influence is acceptable so long as the writer holds the threads to things in his or her own hands. But if the fabric ends up being woven with the materials of others, what then is the meaning of contemporary Persian literature?

If we look at it more generally, the effects of translation have reached the point where a present-day writer or poet pays more attention to the West than to the literary tradition in his or her own mother tongue. It is precisely this level of influence that leads to *gharbzadegi:* western writing techniques, viewing things with western eyes, the selection of western literary form. All of these things, at the same time as they indicate a new birth in Persian literature, have engendered in the reader a feeling of alienation. And if Jamalzadeh and Dashti and Hejazi are still the best-selling authors, it's because they have been less influenced by the new ways and translations. Also, if Hedayat and Nima both appeared out of the blue and at the vanguard of things in their poetry and prose, then it is because they were the pioneers of this new trend. In any case, the future of con-temporary literature will be determined by exactly this modernism, provided the borrowing and imitation does not assume the following guise where, for example, a Persian-speaking writer, unaware of his or her own national and religious mythology, would cling to Greek and Roman myths.

Another point to be made is that contemporary Persian literature pays no attention to style, with respect to geniuneness and clarity of expression, to the forcefulness of language, to succinctness and, in general, to eloquence and stylishness. The majority of poets compose the same sorts of poems, and prose writers write the same way. Very seldom can one infer from a poem or prose piece whose signature should appear at the bottom of it. Of course poets are less inclined to succumb to this defect since the small and fragile vessel of poetry leaves little room for careless omissions or expansiveness. Perhaps this also is a vestige of the influence of the magazines on contemporary literature or of those plentiful translations I've just mentioned. In this context, a point that often meets the eye is the fact that the lesser the responsibility of the pen, the lesser its influence upon the hearts of people, and vice-versa. The consequence of this situation or one of the causes of this defect is writing all kinds of things and trying to do everything. My point has to do with a sort of jack-of-all-trades approach that has become the bane of writers to-day. Everyone of us takes up all kinds of tasks. Since literary criticism does not have its precise meaning as a term, we also end up as critics. I, for example. Because they pay well for translations, we translate too. Because film companies are now doing well, we likewise write scripts. Thus, true specialization has not yet developed in the literary world. All of us do everything. None of us does his or her own special thing. We're in a hurry. We write too much. We're seldom careful. All of these things will definitely ruin our work. We have to be wary of ourselves. Although politics and the university and the age approve of the jack-of-all-trades, literature does not. And as a concluding note, it is certain that contemporary Persian literature has just begun to tread on its own path. It is passing through its own youth. And if it still has its flaws and is not mature, there is no reason to fear. Youthful pride creates pimples on everyone's face.

Translation by Peter Dutz,
The University of Texas at Austin

11

THE OLD MAN (NIMA YUSHIJ) WAS OUR EYES

Al-e Ahmad's forte as a literary critic was his profiles of other Iranian writers. For example, there is his 1951 essay "Hedayat-e *Buf-e Kur*" [The Hedayat of *The Blind Owl*]which is translated in Michael Hillmann, comp. and ed., *Hedayat's 'The Blind Owl' Forty Years After* (1978). Then there is "Samad and the Folk Tale" on Samad Behrangi (1939-1968), which appears in translation as selection 15.

"Pir-Mard Cheshm-e Ma Bud" [The Old Man Was Our Eyes] (1961) was one of several Al-e Ahmad essays on Nima Yushij, the acknowledged father or founder of modernist Persian verse, whose life and works are reviewed by Ahmad Karimi-Hakkak in *An Anthology of Modern Persian Poetry* (1978) and by Leonardo Alishan in "Ten Poems by Nima Yushij," *Major Voices in Contemporary Persian Literature* (1980). A second Al-e Ahmad piece on Nima called "Moshkel-e Nima Yushij" [The Problem of Nima Yushij] examines innovation in his poetry. A third essay is "Nima Digar She'r Nakhahad Goft" [Nima Will Not Compose Poetry Any More], written immediately after the poet's death in January 1960.

Al-e Ahmad's final contribution to the appreciation of Nima Yushij took the form of a question-and-answer session at an evening commemorating the poet in February 1969 at the Faculty of Fine Arts in Tehran. Al-e Ahmad's remarks on that occasion are published in a special commenorative section on Al-e Ahmad in *Nameh-ye Kanun-e Nevisandegan-e Iran*, no. 1 (Tehran: Agah, 1979): 223-253, wherein the Association of Writers of Iran asserts Al-e Ahmad's special significance as a contemporary social critic.

The following is a slightly revised version of the translation appearing in the fall 1974 issue of *The Literary Review*, which also featured a translation of Mohammad 'Ali Jamalzadeh's "Dibacheh" [Preface] to *Yeki Bud Yeki Nabud* (1921), an important manifesto for the modernist, *engage'* literary tradition that Al-e Ahmad later led.

The first time I saw the Old Man was at the First Congress of Iranian Writers which was organized in Tehran by the Iran-USSR Society. July 1946. He quickly came and went. Other poets had nothing to do with him. I was not a poet and, moreover, quite unimportant and only in the crowd by chance. The night it was his turn to recite his poems, I remember the lights went out. They put a candle on the lectern and in that pre-historic atmosphere he recited his "Hey, People." His huge, bald head shone and his eyes and mouth were accentuated. His body seemed smaller and one wondered where that loud voice came from?...Later the first thing I learned about him was from the same short piece published as an autobiography in the Congress' collection. Later on, I searched and found his earlier works in the back issues of *Musiqi* magazine.

Then, when he began to frequent the office of *Mardom*, we became acquainted. He used to come with the same brisqueness, submit his poem, drink some tea, and leave. At first, I'd just exchange greetings with the Old Man, having been introduced by Ehsan Tabari, and later I gradually became bolder and omitted parts of "The King of Conquest" with Tabari's consent. When we published it, there were some bad feelings. It was his first comparatively long and complex poem and the school teachers in the Tudeh Party whose ranks I was to join within the next year didn't understand that "in the total vastness of the night, where this old blackness is dropping the load of his teeth" meant "when the stars faded away on by one." And it was because of this that they huddled around me, asking why? After all, we were called teachers of literature and all that....eventually we met in three sessions and after much discussion, we helped each other understand that one only needs to read Nima's poetry correctly and, for this, must take into consideration his modern punctuation and know how he breaks up traditional metrical patterns and ignores uniformity of line length.

Up to the winter of 1948, I had gone to his house a couple of times. With Ahmad Shamlu. His house was on Paris Street. The runaway poet from Yush in Paris Street, Tehran! Shamlu would read a poem and Nima would sit behind the charcoal brazier, huffing and puffing, and complain about this person or that. And sometimes we'd made a copy of one of his poems and 'Aliyeh Khanom wouldn't show herself and their son, who was a child, was chasing the cat and making noise and every room was carpeted and the manner of the Old Man with his charcoal brazier and smoking paraphernalia had something of the liturgical ritual of the Hindu. Peaceful, careful, and deathly afraid of not finding things in their proper place.

After the split in the Party and the cessation of the journal *Mardom*, I didn't see him again until he and his family had moved to their Shemiran house. Perhaps about 1950 and 1951, I went to see him with my wife once or twice. We had gotten a piece of endowment property from the Ministry of Education in that same neighborhood and we intended to build a nest there. The truth is that if he had not been in that area, that nest would not have been built and we wouldn't have our present home. These comings and goings continued until our house was completed and our neighborly relations began. The area was still a desert and homes sprouted out of the earth. In such a wilderness, an acquaintance meant much. Particularly one with Nima.

It was in those same years that the confrontation between the Third Force and that Party came about. We had brought out three or four issues of *'Elm va Zendegi* when it occurred to me to organize a get-together to win over the Old Man from Tudeh. I did a brief study of his work and took some notes in the same Shemiran house and Reza Maleki, Khalil's brother, prepared his house and invited several people for a session. It was an evening of feasting and the Old Man was really happy and recited a couple of poems and we stayed very late. There were many of us. 'Ali Dashti too was listening to my chattering and Reza Ganjeh'i as well who, when leaving, jokingly said: "Why hasn't he bribed you sooner?" or something like that. Finally. Whatever in that evening tested the tolerance of the crowd came out in the next issue of *'Elm va Zendegi.* Complete with a sketch of the Old Man's face by Bahman Mohasses; the same sketch which encouraged Ziya'pur to go to his house and make a mask of his face which 'Aliyeh Khanom must have now.

Before all these happenings, in 1948 or 1949 when Shamlu reprinted the Old Man's *The Legend,* I made up a piece entitled "The Legend of Nima," which came out in two or three issues in the weekly *Iran-e Ma*. In those days, *Iran-e Ma* was not as empty of everything as it is now and we didn't know that Jahangir Tafazzoli was in the practice of setting one person against the other and enjoying the outcome. Or, at least to increase the sale in the street. What every journalist has learned to do. But I was tricked. That is, the last part of my article hadn't appeared when Partow 'Alavi dived into the ring and, following the same political stratagem of blustering about, he began to insult both me and the Old Man. And I, the untrained debater, wrote something to the newspaper and excused myself from continuing "The Legend of Nima" which in the end had changed to a "Defense of Nima." Because on the other side there was an old man who thought he could achieve total identification on this point alone. Unaware of the fact that looks are indeed deceiving. I remember in that piece I had matched up some of the Old Man's poems with the traditional patterns and had shown his innovations to be not so heretical. The same traditional metrical feet which sometimes appeared as a line of one or two feet and other times as a line of four and a half feet in the various lines. Of course, in my own way, I wanted to simplify the subject for them (the continuation of the same argument I had with my own colleagues) and it was the same subject taken up later by the younger writers. In a book of poetry beginning with "The Amen Bird" of the Old Man, Farhang Farrahi followed the same route. To tell you the truth, this was the way my essay "The Problem with Nima," opened up for me. It wasn't long after these events that the Old Man was trapped by politics again. And his name and signature became a handy slogan for that Party. It wasn't for his own good since he continued to weave his cocoon tighter day by day, and we really didn't expect that; we who were dishing out blows and receiving them in turn, we who lined up on opposite fronts, armed with steel-topped pens. For this reason, I wrote an open letter to him full of politics and blunt candor and he gave a reply which was itself poetry in the same complex prose, fundamentally empty of politics. And to tell the truth I then regretted what I had done. His answer is the best document for understanding his helplessness in politics and explaining why he put himself in anyone's hands. And although both of us ignored these two letters from that time onwards — since I had washed my hands of politics for good and the tide of destiny had crushed the wall which supported him — but anyhow it was the only time we ever stung each other.

From then on, that is after 1953, when we became neighbors, we'd see the Old Man a great deal. Every day in our homes or in the street. He'd be carrying a large brief case and going to or returning from shopping. We'd exchange greetings and ask about each other's health and I wasn't giving the slightest thought to the fact that soon the day would come when he'd no longer be around but I would be. I would sit down and collect some notes about him and, later on, people would discover that in fact I'd collected memories of my own past. Otherwise, that day would come when the Old Man wouldn't be around and, among all the prophets, St. George would be the leader of the band of happy-go-lucky followers and, all by himself, spin an entire collection of poems in one issue of a magazine, using the prestige of their names and poetry and writing the following: "Nima's poetry is confused and often immature..." and no one around to punch him in the mouth!

Sometimes we'd call on each other. Either alone or with our wives. Sometimes to pour out our hearts — sometimes to console him or his wife. About their son who changed his school once a year and we'd do our best to help them understand that it was only a crisis of adolescence and not to worry about it — but it was no use. Or, about their house, whether they should rent it for the summer or not, or about the water ration which was not regular and the water supervisor who was so greedy...and troubles of this sort everyone faces in a new neighborhood and again about their son whom the Old Man had encouraged to rebel and about whom 'Aliyeh Khanom had despaired.

They didn't have an easy life. The Old Man only got a pittance from the Ministry of Education which he'd spend on his huffing and puffing. And 'Aliyeh Khanom who worked for the Melli Bank and got a salary supported the family and looked after the domestic affairs. The Old Man was by himself at home during the day. When 'Aliyeh Khanom retired, things got worse. I've heard several times from her that he wasn't a father, didn't care about home, and put ideas into his son's head...and such gossip as this but there was no other way. The Old Man was only thinking of poetry. Their son was their only child. His father's words had a great effect, the father who ridiculed his son's notebooks and exercises. The Old Man was incompetent in the everyday affairs of living. He was helpless. Basically, he still wasn't used to the urban way of life. After so many years of living in the city, his heart was still in the mountains and he wouldn't hear of living any other way than according to the needs of that life. He wouldn't even buy his own socks. The material for his suit would remain in the tailor's shop for a year. Many times we'd eat together but I wouldn't know what he ate. And what was he living on? He was ill-mannered in eating. He worried about whether the food was by nature cold or hot. He wouldn't eat leftovers. He wouldn't even accept 'Aliyeh Khanom's cuisine. The maid's mouth was always smelly for him and they wouldn't employ a male servant. And on top of all this, his son's sparrows, starlings, and cats were a veritable zoo and the Old Man thought he was eating ten pounds of cat's fur with every mouthful of food. Sometimes, I wondered what he'd do without 'Aliyeh Khanom. He himself knew this quite well. In the last years when they were despairing over their son's schooling, 'Aliyeh Khanom became obsessed with the idea of packing up and taking their son abroad to be as far away as possible from the influences of the father and perhaps become a studious young man. I can't forget how horrified the Old Man was and, one day, he suddenly blurted out, "If they go and leave me alone...?" And lately worse than that both 'Aliyeh Khanom and her son discovered that the Old Man's work was, in fact, not ordinary work.

They discovered they were living with a poet as husband and father. As long as your wife and child are not sure who you are, everything is fine. You are a father and husband, like all fathers and husbands who have responsibilities, and must lighten the family load. If you don't lighten it or even make things worse, there will be words and a quarrel, which of course will or will not soon end in reconciliation. But when your wife and child discover who you are — particularly if as a poet you've left the imitation of Goethe to Khanlari and you're content with being Naser Khosrow or Kleist — then you're in trouble. For your wife and child can't ignore the fact that, more than all these titles, you're still a father and husband and still have all those responsibilities while, alas, being a poet prevents you from fulfilling them. And then they are forced to be proud of you and annoyed with you at the same time. The Old Man was trapped in such circumstances. Especially in the last ten years. And the comings and goings of the young poets just made matters worse. 'Aliyeh Khanom knew the Old Man had become a refuge for the young writers but couldn't stand that much traffic. Especially in that financial situation. He himself was also weary of so many comings and goings but he was unable to do without it, especially since he had acquired some attention so that "Yes, this or that person has taken this or that poem of mine."

The truth is that this or that person would come and insist on getting a poem from him for this or that magazine or newspaper. The Old Man himself would give them a poem and, later, be horrified that they had printed it in their own name or mutilated it. In the latter case, I myself was twice the cause of his horror. Once in the case of "King of Conquest" which I mentioned earlier and the second time in the case of "The Bell" in *'Elm va Zendegi*. He himself was unable to publish his own work. Those who could and did this for him — Shamlu and Jannati — I don't suppose had a pleasant experience doing it. But this was how his work came out regularly and was the cause of more gossip than serious discussion. Instead of putting his work into the hands of others, he put himself. Once, I wrote that he popularized poetry, instead of laying each collection in its proper place like a brick. And I admit here that if I've not intended to give his enemies an alibi to spread gossip. And you see the way I always saw Nima, beyond reach, behind a front, or in a third party's hands. The greatest mistake was that he didn't put himself directly in front of the mirror. There was always a partition, a medium, or some strata. Even his taking refuge in the Party's publications was something like this. He was hiding from the silent conspiracy against him behind the veil of that Party's strength. Especially when the Party's rise coincided with his old age. He was under attack his whole life and was constantly excluded, even from the pages of *Sokhan* whose editor boasted of their close friendship. His only opportunity came in the pages of the Party's publication and for this he was grateful to the end of his days. Furthermore, his brother Ladbon had gone to that side of the world many years ago and was lost and no one knew a thing about him.

I'll never forget when Khanlari who was on the fringes of 'Alam's entourage took the job of vice-minister in the Ministry of Interior. The Old Man came to me one day and said, "Is it possible they'll arrest me because I've destroyed our poetry?"

Of course, he was joking. But he was hiding his horror behind the joke. And when Khanlari was made a senator, his childish terror was doubled. I've seen many people envy others for their artistic achievement in the constricting environment of this wasteland. Even sometimes myself. But he had gone beyond envy and, instead, was horrified. He thought everyone was persecuting him. He seemed to have lived out a lifetime in his "Woe Is Me."

After the events of August 19, 1953, it was natural they would come for him. With that background. He himself sensed this and one day he had brought a sack full of his poems to our house which we left tucked away in the eaves of our home and when the danger passed, returned it to him.

Within the first or second month of those events, they came. One of the well-off persons in the neighborhood who once served as a man-servant in their house had since quarreled with him. After those events, that person had gone and informed them that he possessed a gun but he also had licenses and permits. He had meetings, but what kind of meetings? In fact, they didn't need his gun or meetings in order to arrest him. It was in the morning when they came and searched everywhere. Even inside 'Aliyeh Khanom's powder case. Later, when we met the Old Man, he said, "You're sitting there when suddenly they swarm into your house and go into your wife's bedroom and search for bullets in her powder case. What's the world coming to?"

His life was more or less like this. At noon, when I came back from school, they had taken the Old Man away. 'Aliyeh Khanom was very upset and frightened and didn't know what to do. I realized opium should be sent to him as soon as possible. And while 'Aliyeh Khanom was getting opium from the Tajrish Bazaar, I carried his bedding on my shoulder to the street. There, along the Shemiran Road in front of everyone, I stuffed the pipe into the bedding and set off for downtown. Before reaching the police station, the evening newspapers had come out. In the corner of one of them I wrote in a foreign language where the apparatus could be found and we handed over the bedding at the end of the corridor. We ask Khalil Maleki to look after him; he had been arrested before Nima and had permission for visitors. In the very rooms at the end of the central corridor. Maleki looked after him dutifully. Even before we got there, Maleki had given money to the inmates and they stuck the opium in the pipe for the Old Man and were together every night. But the Old Man couldn't understand what the meaning of this magnanimity was. All his life he lived in poverty and counted his pennies and day by day brooded over the increase in the price of opium. And so when he was freed and Maleki was sent to Falak ol-Aflak, I heard him say, "What a feast! It was as though I had been sent to the sanatorium!"

In a very strange romantic.way, he thought prison without torture was not prison at all. It was in the same years, 1952 or 1953, that Ebrahim Golestan asked once or twice about making a film about him and recording his voice, which was mellow and rich. I thought it wasn't a bad idea. I related this to the Old Man. He couldn't make up his mind. And later on I heard him say, "O yes, these English people want to document me...'

And "these English people" were Golestan who was working for the oil company which had been recently nationalized, and the English themselves were shipped out from Abadan with much ado. He was always like this. He was paranoiac. He couldn't bear the thought of a luxurious life and sometimes seemed petty. I always asked myself if the Old Man had no hardships in life and wasn't afflicted by so much trivia, what then would happen? If he had had a free hand and sat as head of his own magazine and saw other hands stretched out towards him. If he had managed to leave this rustic miserliness in Yush and return, then what would have happened? What would have happened to him, his work, and the result of his work?

Every summer they went to Yush. All of them. They'd rent the house or ask someone to look after it and then assemble everything from sugar and tea to fruits and grains and medicine and a supply of opium. They'd prepare everything and then set off. Just like a trip to Qandahar umpteen years ago! It was a trip to the country and a way of saving money. But I soon discovered that the Old Man in these annual migrations was searching for a remedy to cure the sense of alienation the city had inflicted upon him. I don't know whether he knew it or not but when he came to the city, he wasn't Nima and perhaps he was still the tough cowherd who could ward off death for many years. But when they returned you'd see that the summer in Yush hadn't mitigated his suffering. The Old Man remained a transplanted villager to the end of his life in the commotion of the city. He was an astonished, terrified, and awe-struck peasant! Of course, if they hadn't shut all the doors in his face and in the trap of that conspiracy of silence he hadn't taken refuge in opium which is so relaxing and numbing, perhaps things would have been different. In these last years, one could find the outcry only in his poetry. His gaze was so calm and his movements and life were so untumultuous and his thoughts so peaceful, you'd think he were Solomon standing before the Temple, whose greatness even the legions of demons couldn't find the strength to destroy. But he wasn't always like this.

Many times, I detected terror in his eyes. Especially whenever he fled from the house. And the last time I heard the roar of his anger was one night in our own house. Six or seven years ago. It was a winter night. Irani, Daryush, Fardid, and Ehsani and perhaps one or two other people were there when the Old Man arrived. Tempers were high and everyone followed his own discourse and there wasn't much attention to the uninvited Old Man who at any rate had expectations. Especially at such a gathering. And I don't know what happened or what trivial sting Irani delivered that caused the Old Man to explode. He suddenly stood up and with theatrical gestures cried out so, that all of us were frightened but the content of his cries were so booooohing and his plea for attention so moving I was on the verge of crying. We calmed him with some difficulty. And it was from that night onwards that I knew the Old Man was really helpless. I saw that he too was a man and had trodden the path and lost his strength and then how difficult it became to go and give him support.

I've heard him joke. About Mazandaranis and their manners, about Torkomans, and the physiognomy of this friend or that relative and how clever he was in doing that. Sometimes I even felt that if he hadn't become a poet or if he lived in a larger world, he could have been an actor. He could mimic so well. With all that, when a person, thing, number or concept couldn't fit his usual standard, then he was again the same simple rustic Old Man with his astonishment and helplessness. It was this way the Old Man led a simple life among us far from any pretensions and, with his rustic candor, was continually surprised at everything. The more they harassed him, the tighter he fastened his belt until eventually he resigned himself to all the pettiness of our life. Like a pearl inside a crooked shell closed fast in a dark corner of a far-off shore bank. He had no intention of wandering about the world, no desire for high positions, nor for the beautiful breasts of a woman, nor even a desire for other markets and other customers. He never longed to decorate this stinking bitch of our time with the trappings of false respectability and in his eyes which were the eyes of our generation reigned such serenity that you might think (perhaps correctly) it was a sign of resignation when in fact it was a kind of nobleness you only find in the dim eyes of some statue from pharaonic times.

In all those years we were together I never heard him complain about his body. He was never ill. No headache, no footache, nor any other ache. Opium deceives one quite well. Only once, two or three

years before his death, I heard him complaining. It seems to me it was just before a summer trip to Yush. One afternoon he came to me alone and said promptly, "Do you know, Jalal? My body's no longer capable of doing anything...?

From then on, I became his guardian angel. Whenever I saw him, I'd ask him about a new work or inquire about the revision of an old one. I can truthfully say that it was then he began collecting his quatrains and polishing his "Saqrim Castle."

* * * * * *

The night it happened we were awakened by knocking on the door. At first, I thought it was the water supervisor. Two o'clock in the morning in the winter, this water supervisor was really a half-cocked rooster! When sleep left my eyes, I then understood that it wasn't the pounding of the water supervisor. And I sensed what had happened. "Simin," I said, "I think the Old Man is very sick." It was their maid and she looked frightened.

For some time, the Old Man was ill. for the first time in his life — outside of the world of poetry — he did something unusual. He went to Yush in the winter. And this trip did him in. But he had no symptoms. They had brought him from Yush to the side of the Chalus Road on a mule. His son and a youth about the same size accompanied him. His son said that they had much trouble in bringing him. But he hadn't lost wieght nor had his complexion changed. Only his feet were swollen. And he had difficulty in smoking his pipe. And he talked about a woman they had hired while in Yush who she wouldn't leave when her work was finished. Instead, she would sit and gaze at him like an owl. So much that the Old Man would turn to the wall and pretend to be sleeping. I'm wondering now if that woman had understood, or if the Old Man was hiding his fear of death behind this story. Whatever it was, it was the last interesting thing I heard from him. His last oral poem. He had many of them... Every day or once every two days, we'd call on him. He didn't seem to be dying. He was calm and didn't want anything and looked resigned. And now...?

I threw something over my shoulders and went running. I never thought that everything was already over. I said a doctor should be called or some medicine gotten. 'Aliyeh Khanom was seated at the foot of the *korsi* and held his head against her breast, moaning, "My Nima has gone!"

That big head was hot. But they had closed the eyes. The furnace had been shut down, still, I didn't believe it. But the heart was silent and the pulse had stopped. How hot his big head was!

'Aliyeh Khanom knew better than I that nothing could be done, but she was still restless and kept asking me, "Jalal. Does this mean I've lost my Nima?"

How could you say yes? I sent 'Aliyeh Khanom with Simin to telephone the doctor from our house. The son was sent before my arrival to inform 'Ozamossaltaneh, his brother-in-law. The maid and I helped pull out his body, which was so strangely light, from under the korsi and placed his feet toward Mecca. The terror of death had so widened this young maid's eyes that I realized she couldn't bear it I said, "Go light the samovar. The relatives will be coming soon."

And when she lit the kerosene samovar, I told her to bring the Koran and sent her to Seddiqi who wasn't fond of Nima until the night he heard part of "Saqrim Castle" from the Old Man's very lips in our house. Before Seddiqi came, I opened the Koran. My eyes fell upon the verse:

"By the Angels assembled.."

Translation by Thomas M. Ricks,
Georgetown University

12

THE TALE OF THE SHEPHERD VIZIER

The traditional Iranian folktale with its "once upon a time" premises and allegorical references to Iranian society is another of Al-e Ahmad's modes as a social critic. In fact, his first novel, called *Sargozasht-e Kanduha* [Tale of the Beehives] (1955), was an allegorical depiction in a folk-tale format of exploitation of Iranians and their oil. Then, in *Nun va'l-Qalam* [The Letter 'N' and the Pen] (1961), which may be Al-e Ahmad's best novel, the "once upon a time" narrative techniques is used in an allegory explaining the failure of modern anti-monarchical political movements in Iran. All of this is briefly discussed in Michael Hillmann, "Al-e Ahmad's Fictional Legacy," *Iranian Studies* 9 (1976): 248-265.

"The Tale of the Shepherd Vizier" is really the "Pish dar Amad" [Prelude] and "Pas Dastak" [Epilogue] of *The Letter 'N' and the Pen*. As 'Abdol'ali Dast'ghayb, "Darbareh-ye *Nun va'l-Qalam*" [Concerning *The Letter 'N' and the Pen*], *Ferdowsi*, no. 722 (22 Tir 1965): 8, 14, 16, observes, it is an old Iranian folktale that in part describes the circumstances and factors by means of which those with political power attain their ends.

Once upon a time, there was a shepherd who had a flock of goats and a bald head, which he always covered with an animal skin so that he would not be bothered by the flies. As fate would have it, one day our shepherd was tending his flock on the outskirts of a big town when he came upon a huge commotion. People had poured out of the city to the other side of the moat, carrying flags and banners, each group shouting different slogans or chanting different salutations. Their heads were in the air, their eyes lifted towards the sky.

Our shepherd left his flock in some secure place near a stream in the shade of a mulberry tree, charging his dog to look after them, and went to find out what the commotion was all about. But no matter how long he looked at the sky, he could not see a thing — except for the tops of the battlements and the city gates, decorated with mirrors and carpets. The king's kettle-drum and trumpet band was playing loud enough to deafen the sky itself.

As our shepherd was slowly meandering through the crowd and before he had a chance to ask what was happening, all of a sudden a hand-trained hunting falcon shot through the sky like a meteor and landed on his head. It was one of those falcons that could lift a whole goat up into the air. And before our shepherd could figure out what was what, the people rushed to him, tossed him up over their heads, and whisked him away with cries and salutations. Where to? God only knew. No matter how much he struggled or screamed, the people paid no attention. It had no effect at all. He said to himself, "God, what have I done wrong? What in the world are they going to do to me? Thank God I was saved from that damned animal. It could have gouged my eyes out..." And as he was talking to himself thus, the people passed him over their heads, brought him past the king's stables, right to the king's tent and took him inside. Out of fear for his life, our shepherd took several deep bows, but before he could say, "Your Majesty," the king coughed and held his nose in disgust motioning for him to be taken away and bathed and dressed in fresh clothes before being returned to him.

Our shepherd was utterly confused and also worried about his goats. Again, before he knew what was what, they poured three buckets of hot water over his head and a hefty bath attendant went to work on him. This was all well and good, since our shepherd had not seen the inside of a bathhouse in years. Of course, once in a blue moon if he happened upon a stream, he would take a dip. But, except for his wedding night, he could not remember having been to a bathhouse for a good scrubbing. So, he resigned himself to his fate, pulled the animal skin off his head and set it aside. He then began to get to the bottom of what was going on from the bath attendant, who had never before seen a head like his and was quite dumbfounded. The story was that the week before, some hot lead had apparently found its way into the throat of the king's right-hand vizier, preventing him from breathing. And this was how they were going about appointing his replacement.

Once our shepherd's mind was set at ease, he began to pour out his heart to the bath attendant. Before the business of washing and scrubbing was finished, while they were bringing the ministerial garb to put on him, he learned all the intricacies of the art of viziership from the bath attendant. He memorized all the protocols of the grand, such as "At your service with my life, Your Majesty" and "To the greater glory of Your Royal Highness." And the bath attendant did not fail to perform his duty well; he rubbed down his back thoroughly with warm water to limber up his bones so he could really bow up and down. When the bathing was finished, he put himself in the hands of God and sank into the mantle of viziership.

But, since our shepherd was essentially a man of the hills and mountains and not of the big cities, with their noblemen, kings, and viziers, and since he was basically of a simple nature, a simple, novel idea came to him. When he came out of the bathhouse, he wrapped up his shepherd's vest, his sandals, and the animal skin for his head into a bundle around his shepherd's staff and entrusted it to one of the guards. Upon reaching the ministerial palace, he went first to the cellar and searched and searched until he found an inconspicuous nook, a chest in a closet, in which he put the bundle, locked it up, and put the key in his shawl. Then he set about his task as a vizier, attending to the business of the court.

Now, let me tell you about the cohorts of the former right-hand vizier. With the arrival of our shepherd, their hands were tied and they could no longer live so high on the hog because our shepherd-turned-vizier had cut off their freeloading. He had said, "As is customary in the village, you reap what you sow." Well, dearest reader, these cohorts got together, conspired and schemed and plotted with the left-hand vizier to do in this bumpkin of a vizier who somehow thought that the business of viziership was like being a village headman. So, first they greased the palm of the new vizier's special gatekeeper and, with his help, they eavesdropped, spied on him, and shadowed him until they finally discovered that the new vizier would go to some closet once a week and spend an hour doing something or other in secret. With this tidbit at their disposal, they began to spread the rumor, making sure the king would get wind of it: The king has not been informed, but the right-hand vizier, having just barely arrived, has stored up a treasure vaster than that of Croesus or Solomon, which he has, undoubtedly, stolen from the royal treasury. And, since the king was very just and devoted to his subjects — after all, for this reason, he built twelve new jail-houses every year so that no one would dare to steal or commit any other crime — he agreed with the left-hand vizier that they should go and catch him red-handed and expose him.

Dearest reader, the silver tongued storytellers have related the tale thus: When the appointed day and hour arrived, the king, along with his left-hand vizier, a group of guards and sentries, as well as all the old cohorts, set out — clomp, clomp, clomp — to go to the secret closet of the right-hand vizier. When they sprung open the door and entered, they were so shocked they couldn't believe their eyes. They saw the right-hand vizier, having taken off his ministerial garb, sitting with an animal skin pulled over his head, wearing his shepherd's clothing, leaning against his old, rough staff, and weeping loudly. The king was absolutely in dismay, not to mention the left-hand vizier and the old cohorts.

Well, you can imagine the rest for yourself. After the right-hand vizier was rid of these initial hassles, he dispatched a trustworthy emissary to his ancestral village to pay compensation to the people whose flock had been slaughtered. You see, our shepherd had found out that on that first day, each one of his dying goats had been sacrificed by one or another of the roughnecks of the various quarters of the city as offerings to the king, while the imperial retinue was going by. Having paid his debt, he sent for his wife and children to come to the city. He put his children into school and they lived happily ever after...that is, until divine fate determined that it was time for a new vizier. The right-hand vizier fell out of favor and his food was poisoned at the court banquet. The court physician — who was present and saw what was going on — under the pretext of a diagnosis of colic, ordered him to be taken home immediately. Our shepherd, for whom viziership had brought bad luck, immediately realized what had happened. When he arrived home, he had them lie him down facing Mecca, called his sons to him, and cautioned them never to be lured by the mantle of viziership. He also told them that they should always remember where they had come from. Then, he entrusted them with his shepherd's vest and sandals, lay down his head, and quietly passed away. Since he had neither accumulated any wealth nor saved any money, no one bothered his wife and children. So, after his burial, his wife and children returned to their ancestral plot of land. His daughters married quickly and went away. Their mother did not survive the separation from her husband for more than six months. And the two sons, who had been taking it easy and whose hands were no longer calloused after so long in the city, were not able to pick and shovel and irrigate. So, they sold the plot of land they had inherited from their father and returned to the city. Since they knew no other trade, they started up a school.

Well, dear reader, as we said, after the death of our shepherd vizier, his sons became partners in running a school. But, as the saying goes: If having a partner were such a good thing, God would have taken on one for Himself. The two brothers did not get along. Especially given the fact that running a school was not a profitable business in that day and age. One could barely make a living at it. So, one brother sold his share of the business to a stranger and went in search of the friends and acquaintances that he had acquired at court during the time of his father. He spent all the money he had made from the sale of his share of the school on bribing someone or other and he finally became a court scribe. After passing through all sorts of stages and positions, he was, in the end, appointed the court poet laureate. But the other brother, whose skin was much tougher, managed to remain a school master and eventually, he bought off the stranger's share and became a well-known teacher in the city.

Translation by Mohammad R. Ghanoonparvar,
University of Virginia

13

IRANIAN EDUCATION
AND THE UNIVERSITY

From the early 1960s onward, perhaps the most discussed phenomenon among non-establishment Iranian intellectuals was *gharbzadegi*. The term literally means "the state of being sticken/infected by the West." The person so infected is *gharbzadeh* or "West struck/stricken." Many Iranian writers in the 1960s and 1970s felt that the single greatest danger to Iran's cultural identity, as well as to its ultimate economic and political integrity, was the *gharbzadegi* or "Weststruckness" of many Iranians and the Pahlavi government. Al-e Ahmad popularized the term *gharbzadegi* in a polemic essay by the same name that was written in 1962 and published in basically underground editions thereafter till the late 1970s. Al-e Ahmad's *Gharbzadegi* became much revered by student dissidents throughout the late Pahlavi era.

The selection here is the ninth chapter of *Gharbzadegi* entitled " Farhang va Daneshgah Cheh Mikonand?" [What are Education and the University Accomplishing?] The "Epilogue" (selection 16) includes a translation of the concluding chapter of *Gharbzadegi*. The text for both chapters is *Gharbzadegi*, 2nd revised edition (Tehran: Revaq, 1979). a reputedly "complete and uncensored text" including revisions made by Al-e Ahmad in 1964.

Let's take a look at [Iranian] society from the viewpoint of education... In terms of education, we strongly resemble wild grass. There's a piece of ground; and a seed from somewhere, brought by the wind or in a bird's beak, falls onto it; and the rain likewise helps the grass to grow. In like fashion, we build schools anyway we know how — in order to increase the property value of the surrounding area — or to realize the pretensions of some landowner with clout — or in the name of redressing grievances that such-and-such a tyrant wrought through pillage — or through the sincere efforts of the inhabitants of a village — or by means of the endowment of a third of the wealth of some deceased individual — in whatever form and through whatever means, once the school's built, the apparatus and appurtenances of education also suddenly spring into existence there; and however it happens, one of the fragile and inflexible branches of education reaches the school. Regardless, there's no prior planning in consideration of where what sort of school is needed or what kinds of schools merely provide fun and games. Attention to quantity still prevails over educational wisdom. And the ultimate goal of *gharbzadeh* education is the preparation and deposition of documents attesting to the employment value of education in the hands of persons who are able only to become the future victuals of the bureaucracy and who need documents for promotion to any position. Coordination in the business of schools just doesn't exist. Schools. We have all sorts of them: religious...secular...foreign, and schools that foster spiritual midgets and students of theology. We have technical schools and trade schools, and a legion of other kinds. But nowhere is it entered and recorded what the net result of all this variety is and why all these schools exist and what each of them fosters and for what occupations the products of these schools are being prepared.

And in the programs of all these schools there's no evidence of reliance upon tradition — no trace of the culture of the past — no relationship whatever between home and school — between society as a whole and the individual...schools don't know what they want. But in any event, we have approximately twenty-thousand new high school graduates, and on and on it'll continue...the future victuals of all the worries and pressures and crises and insurrections. Men without faith — void of fire and enthusiasm — the listless tools of the governments of the moment, and all of them a prey. And it is because of this that the theological schools and Islamic educational centers have suddenly come to life and flourished during the past decade, since in these schools at least no one senses danger to the religious faith of the youth. However, what difference does it make since religion and irreligion and education and its lack are the problems of our cities only or are one of the amusements of city-dwellers? For, of fifty-thousand villages in this country, forty-three thousand have no sort of school at all; and would that those villages that have schools didn't, since, in that case, there'd be only one common calamity (i.e., illiteracy); whereas as it stands now, there are thousands of calamitous situations; and each place has a different one.

For instance, at the university which ought to be the most pulsating and distinguished center of research — those university institutes that have to do with technology and applied science... at their most advanced levels of training, merely produce good repairmen for Western manufactures. And those parts of the university that don't concern technology and trades, but deal rather with Islamic studies and Iranian culture..., just as the Islamic religious schools that foolishly assumed that they might, with the preservation of religion and its instruction and propogation, smother the threat of irreligion — which is itself merely one of the symptomatic occurrences of *gharbzadegi* — so the university people assumed that they might, through refuge in Arabism and *belles lettres*, prevent this very same danger. This is why the College of Letters and all its scholars expend their combined energies in the exhumation of graves and in the deep study of things past and in research on about such-and-such and so-and-so. In such colleges, on the one hand, a direct relation to *gharbzadegi* can be clearly seen in this escape into ancient texts and ancient people and the dead glories of literature and mysticism. And on the other hand, there is here observable the greatest and most detestable sign of *gharbzadegi* in the reliance on and involving of orientalists' words that the professors here are guilty of... An educated and compassionate man of traditional upbringing who is likewise a university professor and whose spheres of interest are literature and law studies, when he witnesses how the invasion of the West and how industry and its techniques plunder and carry everything away, this man — can you believe it — supposes the more *Kalileh and Demneh* fables the better! This is why the products of all the literature, law, and theology colleges during the past twenty to thirty years have been so ineffective in society and why, in comparison with the returnees from abroad, they seem backward and out of the main-stream. And may God grant long lives to orientalists who compose an encyclopedia or dictionary for every sort of medieval poem in order to keep the products of our colleges busy and entertained... With very few exceptions the products of these colleges in the past twenty or thirty years have been esteemed scholars the lot of whom (unfortunately) are philologists — all of them with a smattering of knowledge about the famous — all of them idiosyncratic note writers for the margins of other people's books — all of them unravellers of lexical or historical obscurities and — all of them putting in order the graves of the known and unknown dead and demonstrating the intricacies of allusion and plagiarism... — all of them writers of articles about poets in the centuries A.H., whose number doesn't exceed the fingers on two hands. And what's worst of all, most of these persons are teachers of literature, school administrators, and cultural leaders. From this motley group what good or blessing can be expected? Excepting greater submersion into *gharbzadegi*...

A further problem is that of the horde of the European educated or the returnees from America, each and every one of them having returned a candidate for a viziership at the very least, but ending up governmental dead weight. No doubt the very existence of these individuals is a windfall. Yet observe closely and notice what sort of waste and refuse each of these treasures has proved after his return and the opening up of some spot in a ministry and his assumption of some job or other. They find neither the right environment nor have they the requisite ability—they're neither open-handed nor encouraging; and most of them aren't even sympathetic. They are perfect examples of something severed from its roots, this the result of *gharbzadegi*. They are perfect specimens of individuals with their feet in the air. These are the ones who execute the notions and views of foreign advisors and experts. And contrary to the commonly accepted belief, however much the horde of returnees from abroad increases, their power to act diminishes; and the incapacity and disharmony of the organizations that have accepted the influence of the European-trained becomes greater. The reason — on the one hand — there never was a plan in sending these educated youths abroad somewhere to study something. These students, through their own prerogative and initiative, went off, each of them to some corner of the world and studied something and gained some experience that was total distinct and different from the experience of others. And now they've returned. And each one of them must be a cog in a wheel, a member of an enterprise, part of a government organization. Then it becomes apparent how incompatible they are and how incapable and stymied in the performance of any operation. On the other hand, each one of these young men is like à beautiful tulip or narcissus or hycinth whose bulbs we import from Holland and nurture in the greenhouses of Tehran. And after they've bloomed, we buy a flowerpot and bear them as a gift for some friend. And even though our friend puts them in a warm room with sunlight, they don't last more than a week. These choice flowers of our society will likewise wilt from the weather of this region. We've observed them, had experience with them. And should, by chance, they not wither and die, be certain of this fact that they're compelled to go along with the tide. So, contrary to all this propaganda that is expended for the purpose of persuading those college students abroad to return home, I don't feel that the return of these students will offer the prospect of real service to the homeland till the time that an environmental setting is here made ready for their jobs of the future. What is certain is that the people who are going to turn around and advance the life and environment in this intense cold will be those who have both been nurtured in this furnace and adapted to the climate in the cooler. As long as the situation of students going to Europe remains as we see it today [1962], with its present disharmony and the lack of coordination that exists, and as long as the matter of education in Europe is left to individual ingenuity and chance, I don't think there's much hope that the larger the horde of European educated Iranians becomes, the hope of success in the renewal of the structure of our nation will become proportionately greater.

It is because of these particulars that I feel that the time has arrived for us to refrain from sending students to Europe and America. We have seen what results have and have not materialized from all this schooling in Europe and America. The time has arrived when we ought, according to a definite and well laid-out plan for a specific period of time, say twenty years, to send students to Japan and India for university studies and to nowhere else. And if I propose these two countries only, it is ultimately because we know how these two countries have adapted to the machine age and how they've adopted technology and how they've coped with the problems we face. In my opinion, only in the event that such a plan is acted upon, will it be possible through the creation of an equilibrium between the *sharqzadegi* [eaststruckness] of future visitors to Asia and the *gharbzadegi* of present-day returnees from Europe that one can be hopeful concerning the subject of education.

Translation by the editor

14

FIRST DAY IN MECCA

This selection is taken from *Khasi dar Miqat* [Lost in the Crowd] (1966), Al-e Ahmad's *safarnameh* or travel diary of his *hajj* pilgrimage to Mecca in April 1964.

It is the duty of every adult Moslem to perform the *hajj* at least once during his or her lifetime provided he or she has the means to do so. This pilgrimage, which is described in detail in *Encyclopaedia of Islam: New Edition* 3 (1971): 31 - 38, takes place during the first two weeks of the *hajj* month each year in the Islamic lunar calendar and involves set rituals from the moment a pilgrim sets out on the pilgrimage.

Al-e Ahmad refers to a number of important *hajj* terms, rituals and places in this selection, among them the following. *Miqat* which is the place where those planning to enter a *haram* or sanctuary, such as the *hajj* sites, put on the *ihram*. *Ihram* means both the ritual white garment a pilgrim puts on before reaching Mecca and the state of ritual purity a pilgrim so dressed is in. *Muhrim* is the term used to describe the pilgrim in *ihram* and the state of purity. Then there is the focal point of the *hajj*, the Grand Mosque of Mecca, in whose precincts are located the rectangular Kaaba building that pilgrims circumambulate, the black stone they kiss, and the well of Zamzam whose water they drink. In Arabic, it is often referred to as al-Bayt al-Haram [the sacred house], and in the English text here as the "House" or "House of God."

After ceremonies in the Mosque area are completed, *hajj* pilgrims perform a ritual *sa'y* or walk and run along a street called Mas'a between two hills in Mecca called Safa and Marwa. They begin the course by walking and then increase the pace to a *harwalah* and then a run, covering the course seven times.

From the perspective of pre-Khomeini Iran, Al-e Ahmad's *hajj* pilgrimage and the personal acceptance of Islam it signified·might seem a strange gesture on the part of a modern, nationalistic, Western-style intellectual. But, in hindsight from the perspective of the overwhelming rejection of Pahlavi westernization that took place in Iran during 1978, Al-e Ahmad's *hajj* appears symptomatic of the turning of some Iranian intellectuals away from western secularism, as Nikki Keddie argues in "Iran: Change in Islam," *International Journal of Middle Eastern Studies* 11 (1980): 535.

Saturday, 18 April 1964
Mecca

We got to Mecca at 4:30 in the morning. We left Medina last night at 8:30. Our vehicle was a bus — one of those red ones — whose top had been removed. The passengers took their places in the bus at 5 in the afternoon. Then there was a very long wait, until 8 o'clock, when Javad came and called me. I got stuck with a bad seat, on the third row, next to my uncle. I was the third person in a two-person seat. The driver was a good man. His bus was in good condition, and our guide was claiming he had greased his palm. And so we came directly here, with only one stop in Rabigh, and another one at the beginning of the trip at the Haflah mosque, where we made ourselves *muhrim*. In the dark of the night. There was no water and no privy. We performed the ritual purifications in the light of the bus's headlights. We had already put on the *ihram* garments in Medina, followed by the mosque rituals, getting back on the bus, and riding on and on and on. The sky and stars overhead were very low, the sky was amazingly close, Scorpio was right in front of us, and the wind blew in our faces constantly (some eighty to one hundred kilometers per hour). We were huddling all the time. Then there was the responsibility of looking after my uncle, an old man who was continually nodding off and in danger of hitting his head on the back of the seat in front of him. Never have I spent a night so awake and so mindful of nothing.

Under cover of that sky and in that infinity, I recited every poem I'd ever memorized — mumbling to myself — and looked into myself as carefully as I could until dawn. I saw that I was just a "piece of straw" which had come to the *miqat*, not a "person" coming to a "rendezvous." I saw that "time" is an "infinity", an ocean of time, and that *miqat* exists always and everywhere, and with the self alone. A "rendezvous" is a place where you meet a person, but the *miqat* of time is the same kind of meeting of the "self." I realized how beautifully that other infidel Bayazid Bestami had put it when he told that *haji* bound for the House of God at the gates of Nishabur, "put your sack of money down, circumambulate around *me,* and go back home." I realized that traveling is another way of knowing the self, of evaluating it and coming to grips with its limitations and how narrow, insignificant, and empty it is, in the proving ground of changing climes by means of encounters and human assessment.

Same day at *Bayt al-Haram*

It appears that even the Kaaba will have been rebuilt with steel reinforced concrete by next year, just like the Prophet's Mosque. Not only has the Mas'a between Safa and Marwa been transformed to a huge two-layered cement passageway, they are also already busy putting in a new rectangular two-story outer corridor, thereby destroying the one built by the Ottomans. They've already taken out one side of the old outer corridor, the one facing the Mas'a, and they will undoubtedly destroy the other parts of it within a year or two. It's true that the space available for circumambulation will be wider and that a larger crowd — three or four times the size of the current one — will be able to circumambulate the Kaaba, but the problem is that they will be using these cement slabs attached to reinforced concrete pillars, and building upward with them...With beautiful hard rock close at hand, still they always use this cement and cement forms. The way it looks, the only thing that will be left of the old outer corridor will be two or three minarets. They've covered the circumambulation track around the Kaaba with marble, and those in the covered corridors as well. There were more people on the run between Safa and Marwa than there were making the circumambulation. As soon as the sun gets hot the circumambulation virtually ceases.

I'm now sitting on the second level of the outer corridor, writing. From up here the Kaaba is just half the size I had imagined. That devotee of God who was the architect of this new outer corridor was evidently unaware of the fact that when you destroy proportion you change the architecture. The Kaaba is still the same size, but they've made the outer corridor twice as wide, and twice as high. How about destroying the Kaaba itself and making it higher and larger? Out of reinforced concrete, no doubt? (A tall, fat, swarthy man carrying an umbrella just passed, saying "Haji sir, mention me in your journal too

— Qandahari of Mashhad." 'Sit down', I said, though there was a hint of mockery in his voice. It seems that this sort of activity is distastefully ostentatious in this setting, though I've so far seen two or three others writing on paper, note pads, or what-have-you myself. I must be more careful after this. (Out in public and writing?)

Afternoon. Same Day.
Mecca.

The House our guide procured for us is in the Sulaymaniyah district, in Northern Mecca at the foot of Mount Hindi. It's really a three-story house with three large rooms. The women are crowded together on the first floor, the men on the other two. The owner of the house himself and his wife and children are temporarily living on the roof. Our guide says the guy works in the Mecca treasury offices. Money managers are the same the world over. Yes indeed. That gentleman Sayyed Borujerdi and his followers, who've now become a tight little group, have gone to the upper floor, and we constantly hear their calls to prayer, their *rowzehs*, and their mournful eulogizing. The rest of us, who are less fanatical, and do not think ourselves in need of *akhonds* and mullahs, are here on the middle floor. My sister has gone to be with the women. There are four of us left in my family with several people from our neighborhood back home, eight or ten Mazandaranis, and a villager from Sagzabad who insists on saying he's from Tehran. He's always trying to hide his accent. Worse yet, he's always trying out foreign cigarettes, and as a result he coughs all the time. The house has a bath house, which was immediately converted into a pantry. There's a shower on every floor, with a privy. Our floor also has a small room with a sash window of colored glass, which was taken by the Isfahani family. Our roomates have deprived us here in Mecca of the privileged status we had in Medina. They are three women and three men, all of them young. On both sides of our room at the base of the wall are high, interfacing wooden trunks that line up in bench-like fashion. We let the old people and those who are spoiled sleep on those. The rest of us roll up in our blanket on the floor. We all eat from the same undivided *sofreh* cloth spread over the floor.

The old Mazandarani man, who looks just like Nima Yusij, and has his picky eating habits, behaves for all his years just like a child. For whatever reason, he left his fellow Mazandaranis in a huff at lunch, taking his plate to a corner of the room. After lunch he said,

"You educated people! What would you say is the difference between a round prayer and a linear prayer?" (The words seemed to be
sloshing in water in his mouth as he spoke). And of course we didn't
know. Then he explained that a round prayer is the one offered by
the people assembled around the Kaaba, and a linear prayer is the
one they offer at his village mosque. It turns out that on his first encounter he had become deeply involved in the Kaaba experience.
After him the others began telling stories, recalling *hajj* incidents and
exchanging friendly banter. Everyone is obviously feeling rested
now.

Mecca has more mountains around it than Jerusalem, and the
city is largely made of stone. So much granite! No wonder the pre-
Islamic Arabs had crammed so many statues into the "House"! *Bayt
al-Haram* sits in a depression right at the bottom of the drainage area
between the mountains. The water of Zamzam is a kind of reservoir
for the rainwater that runs off these granite mountains and collects in
that channel. The streets go up and down, mostly following the
valleys, with homes on both sides going up the sides of the mountains, and you find another flank of the mountain in every corner,
with another neighborhood and another street. The streets have
neon lighting, and there are multi-colored mini-skyscrapers along the
streets, with garish coloration in the new windows, such as bright
green and burgundy... Very primitive, and it badly defaces the city.
There are enough garages and motels to satisfy anyone, and then
shops, shops, and more shops. They've torn down everything all
around *Bayt al-Haram* in order to build a square which is not yet
completed, and dirt is piled up all around in heaps and pits. Hajis
come and go in the midst of the remaining construction equipment.
To build something in this city, there's no need to dig and pour a
foundation. No matter how high a building is to be, it may be laid
right on a natural stone base and raised from there, except in the
depression in the city's center where *Bayt al-Haram* is located. It's
really in the middle of a big bowl that has a flat layer of sand on the

bottom. They've dug a thick foundation there for the new corridor,
and the reinforced concrete forms are still in place. The entire
Eastern side of *Bayt al-Haram* is joined to the city by a continuous
network of wood and iron construction scaffolding.

The first thing in the morning when we reached the gates of
Mecca we were welcomed by a kaliedoscopic fountain that sprayed

water three to four meters into·the air in the center of the square at the gate. I wished Maham could be there to see it, and have the happiness of knowing that they're using the colors he likes all over the world. Neon fills the streets everywhere. It's even on top of the House's minarets and the Kaaba itself. When it pleased God to have a house built on the surface of this land, he should have realized that that land would one day fall into the hands of the Saudi government, and that its doors and walls would be covered with neon because of the exigencies of oil exportation. I'm not advocating replacing the neon with kerosene, but, for dignity's sake, why shouldn't they order specially designed lamps from these companies that would be worthy of such grandeur, and not have even the House of God become a common consumer for Pennsylvania? Doing things this way means tainting even the world of the unseen for company profits.

Another item. I visited the infirmary this morning. It was quite crowded. There was a lot of sunstroke and diarrhea. The bald head of one of our Esfahani fellow travellers was so blistered it frightened me. I got some Sulfoguanidine and left. I'm still on a restricted diet. Tea and compote. My gripes and stomach pains ended before we left Medina with the help of several Bladons pills. I showered in the afternoon, in the shower above the sump in the privy. I ran the water over my head. Two or three of my fellow travelers saw me, and looked at me with unspeakable disgust, with looks that said, "You'll be ritually impure!" and so on. They said nothing, however. After all, an important concern on such a journey is the enjoinment and prohibition of others, of good and evil...

At lunch — served on a common spread (I think we are now about twenty more than we were) — we had watermelon, *paludeh* noodles, and bread and cheese. I opened a can of the compote. I put a bit of lemon juice on it so I could eat it. I can't stand sweets. Also abruptly stopped drinking water today. Tea, tea, tea.

Same day. Saturday.
Mecca.

This sa'y between Safa and Marwa stupefies a man. It takes you right back to fourteen-hundred years ago, to ten-thousand years ago, (it isn't hopping, it's simply going fast) with its *harwalah* pace, the loud mumbling, being jostled by the others, the self-abandon of the people, the lost slippers — which will get you trampled underfoot if you go back for one moment to recover them — the glazed stares of the crowd, which is chained together in little groups in a state not unlike a trance, the wheelchairs bearing the old people, the litters borne by two people, one in front and one behind, and this great engulfing of the individual in the crowd. Is this the final goal of this assembly? And this journey...? Perhaps ten-thousand people, perhaps twenty-thousand people, performing the same act in the same instant. Can you keep your wits in the middle of such vast self-abandon? And act as an individual? The pressure of the crowd drives you on. Have you ever been caught in the midst of a terrified crowd, fleeing from something? Read "self-abandon" for terrified, and substitute "wandering aimlessly" "seeking shelter" for fleeing. One is utterly helpless in the midst of such a multitude. Which one is really an "individual?" And what is the difference between two-thousand and ten-thousand? Each of the Yemenis, filthy, with tangled hair, sunken eyes, and a rope tied around the waist, looks like another John the Baptist risen from the grave. The blacks, heavy, tall, and intense, froth on the lips, moving with all the muscles of their bodies. A woman with her shoes under her arm runs, crying like someone lost in the desert. Whatever they are, they don't seem to be human beings to whom one may turn for help. A strong, smiling young man collides with someone and moves on, like a fool in a frenzied bazaar. An old man, panting, is unable to continue, but he is swept on by colliding bodies. I realized I could not watch him be trampled by the people. I took his hand and guided it to the rail in the middle of the runway that separates those coming from those going back. A group of women (there were twelve to fifteen of them) wearing the white *ihram* garments, had marked the backs of their necks — violet flower designs — and each held onto another's *ihram* by the waist band. They were moving in one line towards the circumambulation.

You see the ultimate extent of this self-abandon at the two ends of the Mas'a, which are a little elevated, and at which you must go around and return. The Yemenis jump and spin every time they get there, say "salaam" to the Kaaba, then start again. I realized I couldnt' do it. I began to cry and fled. I realized what a mistake the infidel Mayhanah'i of Bestami made by not coming to throw himself at the feet of such a crowd, or at least his selfishness... Even the circumambulation fails to create such a state. In the circumambulation around the House, you go in one direction shoulder to shoulder with the others, and you go around one thing individually and collectively. That is, there's an objective and a system. You're a particle in a ray of being going around a center. You are thus integrated, not released. More importantly, there are no encounters. You're shoulder to shoulder with the others, not face to face. You see selflessness only in the rapid movement of the bodies of people, or in what you hear them saying. In the *sa'y* however, you go and come, in Hagar's same wandering manner. There's no aim in what is being done. In this going and coming, what's really troublesome is the constant meeting of eyes. A haji performing the *sa'y* is a pair of legs running or walking rapidly, and two eyes without a "self," or that have leaped out of the "self," or been released from it. These eyes aren't really eyes, but naked consciences, or consciences sitting at the edge of the eye sockets waiting for the order to flee. Can you look at these eyes for more than an instant? Before today, I thought it was only the sun that could not be regarded with the naked eye, but I realized today that neither can one look at this sea of eyes...and I fled. After only two laps. You can easily see what an infinity you create in that multitude from such nothingness, and this is when you are happy, and you've just begun. If not, in the presence of such infinity you see how you are less than nothing. Like a particle of rubbish on the ocean, no, on an ocean of people, or perhaps a bit of dust in the air. To put it more clearly, I realized I was going crazy. I had an urge to beat my head against the first concrete pillar and break it open. Unless you do the *sa'y* blind.

When you leave the Mas'a there is a bazaar, with people packed tightly together. I sat in a corner with my back against the wall of the Mas'a. I was quenching my thirst for one of these "colas" and thinking of something I'd read by a European on the problem of the "individual" and society, and that the greater the society that envelops the "self", the nearer the "self" comes to being nothing. I realized that the Eastern "ego" that forgets itself and its troubles in such a state of equality in the presence of the world of the unseen is the same one that, in the ultimate individualism of seclusion, claims to be divine. Just like that infidel Bayazid Bestami, and others. The Joks of India as well. I realized that this "ego" is sacrificed in isolation just as much as it "sacrifices itself" in society. At its highest levels of satisfaction, what is the ultimate attainment of Yoga if not this? To give peace of mind over to asceticism, for if one is nothing in the manifest world of action outside the self, one can at least impose the design of one's will on one's body! Therefore, what is the difference between existentialism and socialism? In the *sa'y* we escape our confinement, and we do something that is to "our" benefit, whether in the mind or in reality. In Yoga, we remain in "self" confinement, which is to say that since we have no power to act outside the body, we settle for the small, weak domain of our bodies. In the sa'y, we accept society's domination, but only in the presence of the world of the unseen. If you came and took the "world of the unseen" out of this multitude, what would be left? In our system, neither the individual nor society has priority. Priority goes to the world of the unseen, which is connected to the bazaar, and has come under the control of companies. The individual and society are two transient phenomena in contrast with something that signifies eternity: but they are two sides of the same coin. It is only in such a domain that "ayatollah" and " zelollah" [The Shadow of God] have meaning.

Both individually and as a society, we have closed the door to the manifest world of action. When a meaning is found for the relationship between the individual and society, whether by the individual or by society, you move in the direction of manifestion and action, or society does. Just like that Da'i Qobadiyani. Otherwise, we've been doing the sa'y for fourteen-hundred years, and for a thousand years we've had isolation, seclusion, and martyrdom, but not for the sake of manifesting anything. This is the opposite of self-sacrifice. This self, if it doesn't exist as a particle working to build a society, is not even a "self". It is absolutely nothing. It is that piece of rubbish or particle of dust, except (and a thousand exceptions) when it exists in the context of a great faith, or a great fear. Then it becomes the builder of everything from pyramids to the Great Wall of China, and even China itself. This goes for the entire Orient, from the Fall of man until today.

With these futile ideas in my head and my thirst for a "cola" purged, I went looking for the Zamzam well. They had brought the mouth of the well below the surface, right beside the House. There are wide steps in the middle of the square taking you down. Then there is a corridor with pipes along the walls on both sides and a spigot every two steps. At every spigot three or four people are holding pails, pans, and canteens, waiting for a turn. Then you come to a door leading to the mouth of the well, through which women are not allowed. And what could be better? Such commotion! Like a men's bathhouse, all of them soaked in water and sweat, the well in the center with a tall, thick, cylindrical mouth and three pulleys above it attached to the ceiling, each one dangling a rope into the well and buckets being raised and lowered in turn. Is it possible, however, to distribute the water without wasting it? The pails the hajis have brought for bearing the water have lids, and on each lid is a narrow screw-on cap, so they can take the well water back home uncontaminated. In all that crowding, rushing, and scuffling, how can one pour a narrow stream of water from the big well buckets into such little holes? I waded slop slop through the water, made one round with difficulty, and came out. *Ihrams* were clinging to everyone, and there was a kind of good-natured quarreling going on among all of them, as they reached ahead of each other to take the water buckets and empty them into their souvenir buckets. God save us from the police, who are everywhere, with their hats, badges, and pistols. One of them stood at the mouth of the well just watching the operation of the pulleys. His clothes clung to his body and water dripped all over him. He held his pistol to his side with one hand and fanned himself with the other. There were two to three aggressive hajis standing at the mouth of the well drawing up water and pouring it on the other people. Just like a bathhouse. What would it be like if you didn't see the trademarks, emblems, and weapons at the mouth of the Zamzam well and you forgot that there too you're under government control? Even on the *hajj* there's not a moment's opportunity to evade this ugly, unavoidable reality. Oh yes. Unless the *Hajj* rites were to be brought under international Islamic control, and so on.

It's quite a spectacle when the people are poising themselves outside the Kaaba or beneath a portico for the circumambulation. The guide gives instructions; and the others, who have already worked out some arrangements among themselves listen attentively. Holding onto one another's hands, *chadors*, or *ihrams*, they start out, walking in place at first, and then swarming ahead. I'm certain, however, that they become dispersed and scattered at the very outset. Each one in the multitude goes in a different direction, and each loses his way going home and spends a half day wandering around aimlessly. The women are really just spectators in these rites. They're not admitted to the graveyard, nor to the shrines of Uhud and Zamzam. Tonight, on the second floor above the Mas'a between Safa and Marwa, there were a number of them in front — at the edge of the roof — having taken places for the prayer. They were quite happy, watching the "House" and the circumambulation around it, when two of three Torkamans came up and convinced them that the women ought to get behind the men. And they did it.

Then there are these huge cloths they spread out underfoot! First they soak them with water from the Zamzam well, then spread them out beneath the hajis' feet, end to end, over the House of God's marble carpet and over the hot sand (the marble carpet over the floor of the mosque is not yet completed) both to prevent the hajis from burning their feet and to bless the cloth as a commodity for the next life. Apart from the *ihram,* which everyone keeps, the greatest souvenir the hajis bring back is a burial shroud.

I then went up on the Eastern roof and kneeled to pray in a place at the roof's edge overlooking the entire House and the surrounding area. The call to prayer came at 6:20, later than the usual Medina time. As the call arose, the crowd circumambulating the Kaaba, moving toward the center from the edges, began to quiet down and form circular ranks. By the time the words *allahu akbar* [God is great] were heard, the entire mosque population was in concentric files. The last circumambulators lined up in the twinkling of an eye, but there was still a flurry of activity in that corner where the black stone sits in one of the Kaaba's walls as I began my prostrations. By the time I raised my head again the entire mosque population was lined up, from one end of the porticos and rooftops to the other. The greatest assembly of human beings under this sky who come to gather in one place in response to a command. There must be some meaning to this gathering! A meaning higher than this dealing, marketing, tourism, discharge of obligation and ritual enactment, economy, government, and a thousand other inevitable things! When the prayer reached the second *salam* there was a sudden explosion of people from that corner in front of the stone, rushing to kiss it. Then the prayer ranks broke and the circumambulation began anew. At first the ranks nearest the Kaaba arose and started circling, then those behind them followed in a stately rippling motion moving away from the center. The gentlemen who built these new arched porticos were aware of the grandeur of their task, but it's a pity. And God save us from all these reinforced concrete molded structures. Despite this, when it's finished it will be the largest uncovered temple on earth, with two new monstrous minarets competing with each other to be the highest.

As I descended the steps I suddenly realized my foot was burning painfully. I withdrew into a corner and bent over to find the cause of the burning. I saw that there were new blisters. Then I looked at my shins and saw that they were covered with strange red blemishes, and it continued higher up. I hiked my up *ihram*. It was on my chest and belly too, as well as my arms. Because of my bad liver and this hot sun. As I straightened up to leave I caught a woman raising her eyes and looking me over.

Translation by John Green and Ahmad Alizadeh,
University of Michigan and Portland State University

15

SAMAD AND THE FOLK LEGEND

Samad Behrangi (1939-1968) was a teacher, educational reformer, folklorist, and children's story writer who died under circumstances that raised the suspicions of anti-Pahlavi Iranians that he had been assassinated.

Behrangi's life and works have been reviewed in Michael Hillmann's introductory note to a translation of Behrangi's preface to *Kand-o Kav dar Masa'el-e Tarbiyati-ye Iran* [An Investigation of Educational Problems in Iran] (1965) in *Major Voices in Comtemporary Persian Literature — Literature East and West* 20 (1976): 196-198; and in Gert J. J. de Vries' brief biobibliographical essay in *Encyclopaedia of Islam: New Edition, Supplement* (1981): 135. Some typical Behrangi stories appear in translation in *The Little Black Fish and Other Modern Persian Stories* (Washington, D.C., Three Continents, 1976), a volume reviewed by de Vries in *Major Voices*, pp. 323-327.

Al-e Ahmad's "Samad va Afsaneh-ye 'Avam [Samad and the Folk Legend] was written in November 1968 and published in the special Behrangi commemorative issue of *Arash*, no. 18 (Nov./Dec. 1968), which has gone through several subsequent printings. Behrangi himself remains a hero for many politically active Iranians, particularly those opposed to the establishment of an Islamic Republic in Iran.

In this very allusive essay, Al-e Ahmad refers to one person whose significance needs some explanation here. That is Gholamreza Takhti (1930-1968), an Iranian Olympic champion wrestler and folk hero. Many Iranians became convinced that

Takhti's death, announced as suicide by the Pahlavi government, was a political assassination prompted by his immense popularity and personal integrity. Takhti's funeral at Ebn-e Babuyeh in Tehran was a major political event of the 1960s.

When the news of my older brother's death arrived from Medina, my father said in a loud voice: *la ilaha illa Allah*, and nothing more. He didn't even cry, but repeatedly said, "There is no god but God." Not once. Not ten times. Repeatedly! Could it be that he did this so as not to lose his mind? When a newcomer would arrive to express his sympathies, or you said hello, or the kids took some tea to him, instead of responding or speaking of anything else, he would repeatedly say: *la ilaha illa Allah*.

Until Tuesday night arrived. The night of our *rowzeh*. Then he wept. And how he wept! We had never seen him cry over the tragedy of Karbala in such a manner. Especially since the preacher on that night was an intimate, and he spoke of [Hosayn's son] 'Ali Akbar and of the father's presence over the son's corpse, of the breaking of his back, and all the other things... But when the *rowzeh* was over, again there was nothing more but the same, "There is no god but God." He had even forbidden my mother and sister to weep aloud. But he never dyed his beard with henna or shaved his head again. The barber would come to our house and cut his hair very short. And from then on, he would always carry his cane. Before that he only took his cane when he wanted to go to an important gathering. But after that, the cane never left his hand.

And so it was until my brother's wife and child returned from Medina and we found out that he had died suddenly and of an unknown illness. One night he had gone to a party at a friend's house, had returned late, and had gone to bed. In the morning, he had not awakened. That was it! But how could anybody believe that? At least if there had been talk of some illness, or bad food, or complaint from a chronic pain — anything! But his wife and son were present and there had been no talk of any of those things. Father's disciples would come and go, from this gathering of mourners to another, from the mourning ceremonies of this neighborhood to the other, until, at last, it was found — a pretext was found! "So-and-so who had come from Karbala, quoting so-and-so who had returned from Medina, had said, the Sunnis poisoned so-and-so!" And it became a belief. To be the representative of the *marja'-e taqlid* in Medina and to be as active as my brother had been and not to ever have complained of an illness and then to suddenly die?! It's true that death makes no announcements, but... and a thousand other buts, each the conversation topic of one of father's close circles. By now everyone was positively sure that my brother had been poisoned. The bewilderment of one, another's regret, the astonishment of a third, a fourth's disbelief, the desire of a fifth to see him once more, all found expression in this same hearsay rumor so that oblivion and normalcy might return and they might be delivered; so that they might make a saint of a man asleep at the feet of the four Imams in the cemetery at Medina, who has had your flesh and skin, and has suffered for the sake of the happiness of others.

And now the agony of the news of this younger brother's death, the agony of Samad. The news came from the Aras River, from the Khoda Afarin area. And how revealing names are! Sa'di gave me the news. Over the telephone. "Hello" and "how are you" in a choked voice; the kind that you hear in the company of an intimate friend, or over a drink and a talk. Then, "Samad has fallen into the Aras!" which I heard as 'araq [vodka]. Probably because his voice was so choked, or maybe because the news was so unexpected. After all, we're more used to hearing this other one — that so-and-so has fallen into heroin, and so-and-so has fallen into the lap of the establishment, and another, into the infernal well of a mercenary. And now, Samad too. But he wasn't into these things! He had harder bones than that. A wandering peasant from "Khosrow Shah" and "Mamaqan" and "Dehkharqan." A gypsy...No, an *'asheq* [minstrel] in the Azarbayjani sense of the word. An *'asheq* whose *tar* the *millat* [the people] carried on its shoulders, I mean Behruz [Dehqani] did. No, *'araq* shouldn't have felled him. That's all I said in response to Sa'edi. And also, "Let's get up and go to Tabriz. Let's go to him. We'll publish his *Alphabet* ourselves. You know how much they've made him suffer..." when Sa'edi said, "They recovered his corpse three days later..." I froze and sat down. "And what else?" Well, he had gone to relax by the water with a friend, who knew how to swim. He had been collecting stories around that area. And I guess, sometimes he went there just for fun. But he didn't know how to swim himself. And he had fallen in. His friend had returned alone, hitting himself over the head. Now they've arrested a number of his acquaintances in Tabriz. And in answer to the interrogations, his friend has picked up a chip-axe and has hit himself over the head. And other things as well... But is that all? And this is supposed to mean that Samad is dead? The same for whom we had so many dreams in our heads? This village language of Azarbayjan — this wakeful conscience of an exiled culture — this toddling fellow-traveller of Hans [Christian] Andersen — this mobile teacher who had stepped out of the lines of [Shahriyar's] *Haydar Baba Salam* and was escaping to Savalan and Khalkhal?

But what if they've finished him off? What if he has committed suicide? Or else, why would a man who doesn't know how to swim, get into the river? And, anyway, how much water does Aras hold during early September to enable it to overpower a man? I've seen the riverbed in Pars Abad. It's not located in a position where one could get into it without being bothered by the border guards on either side. And the river has a wide breadth and each spot has a shallow crossing, no deeper than Sefid Rud at the foot of Imamzadeh Hashem. And on the heights of bothsides there are fences of barbed wire with guards standing watch. But they said his friend was a young officer. So, I guess, he had taken care of the border guards through the authority of his uniform. And then they said that in Khoda Afarin, the riverbed grows narrow and the pressure of the water...etc. But I still can't believe it. Is it because of a kind of subjective romanticizing? An escape from reality? Or another act of folkloric legend making? I don't know. I only know that — hey, Manaf! It's you I'm talking to! — I only know that Samad should not be dead! Samad cannot be dead!

I came to know Samad though his *Investigation of Educational Problems in Iran*. Meaning, I heard the groan of a kindred spirit. And, to be honest with you, it made me very happy. To see that someone from the other end of Azarbayjan is saying the same nonsensical things makes you believe, even it it's only for a day, that what you've been saying wasn't so nonsensical after all!... And then I followed him through his stories. And later, when he would sometimes appear briefly in Tehran. Then we went to Tabriz in the spring of 1967, with Sa'edi. Samad was there, and so were Behruz and the other Behruz and Kazem. And there were those nights filled with sincerity and fervor and the 'asheqi songs of Behruz and the breakfasts at the coffeehouse of "Qoleh" and the talks that finally led to *Tarh-e Tabriz* [The Tabriz Sketch] which Sa'edi and I completed upon our return. And thinking we could still ask, from that "saint" of

"Social Researches" for a miracle, we gave it to those gentlemen. What a shame! To cast one's pearls for the hundredth time before the s... before the scholars! The real movers of that sketch were Samad and Sa'edi. A sketch for the revitalization of a city to which, all of us throughout Iran, owe so very much. And Samad had his contribution to that sketch already prepared. I mean, his *Alphabet*. With what patience he had sat down and prepared a first grade reader with a combination of Persian and Turkish (which we've been told to call "Azari"!) words so that Azarbayjani children might not be forced to write the Turkish *su* [water] and *chorak* [bread] and the Persian *ab* [water] and *nan* [bread], without understanding why? It's true that the sketch did not pull any weight with the Western inclined scales of that institution and was filed away, however, Samad's *Alphabet* arrived which I took to the appropriate public office along with a couple of words introducing the author, saying, "He's a poet and sensitive. Take care not to meddle with his book," and other things of the sort. Their argument was that after all, it needed a method, pictures, vowelling, etc. I said, "How about asking him to come to Tehran?" Which they did, and Samad came to Tehran from Khosrow Shah. Then they settled to editing the book and to making it relevant to the times. Consequently we had an opportunity for more visits and talks. Once he came with one of his stories and with his folkloric poem inscribed as a dedication on the first page:

> Darling, comb in the garden,
> Undo your hair and comb it in the garden.
> They've hanged the nightingale in the garden
> For the sake of the flower.

Which made me realize how romantic he was and, at the same time, how insistent he was in revitalizing his mother tongue — meaning, beware of the presence of this separating sickle which is Aras along with other bisecting elements — whose presence we have not tolerated in our schools and culture for the past fifty or sixty years. Another time he was at a party where two or three university professors were present. Because of Samad's presence, the discussion shifted towards the Turkish language, which made me realize how bold he was, how fiery, and how sharp! I had thought that only I had these qualities!

Another time we went with Sa'edi to Ebn-e Babuyeh. The three of us had something to eat at one of the kabob stands at the entrance of the Shah 'Abdol'azim bazaar, parked the car in a corner, and cast ourselves into the crowd. And what a crowd! The poor, the laborers, the man on the street, and once in a while, bazaar merchants and office clerks. And all, young. And then the pavilions, the groups, the banners, and the lamentations. The printed elegies that were being distributred, and the voice from the loudspeaker saying, "Gentlemen, some people have fainted around the tomb. It's dangerous. Make way so that they may be carried into open air..." And then the plaintive poems and verses from the Koran and *rowzeh* and mourning the agony of 'Ali Akbar, and the women sitting on a bench or on a balcony and brewing tea. Then a woman wearing a veil and carrying a child in her arms said hello to Sa'edi. Sa'edi picked up and kissed the child. Then they casually inquired about each other's health, and we left, having discovered that she had given birth to that child a couple of years ago and that the navel cord had been wrapped around the child's throat and had almost strangled the child, by the time the doctor had arrived. Then we stood on top of a gravestone and watched the groups pass by and the crowds of people squirming about. And we were thinking how released unto itself is such a crowd! And what power and what waste! When two young men came and stood beside us, I was trying to transcribe the lamentations, but with each newly-arrived group, a new lamentation would arise.

Then one of the young men said, "When will this *Two-Year Report* of yours be published?"

I said, "I think it will be a three or four-year report. I don't know." And then I asked them, "How large do you estimate this crowd to be?"

The first one said, "Eighty thousand. One-hundred thousand..."

And the second one said, "The statistics could be taken."

And Samad said, "Come off it! Leave statistics to the scholars."

The first young man said, "Worshipping the dead has become widespread again."

I said, "It was widespread. From a very long time ago."

Sa'edi said, "What's wrong with it? It's still *something!*"

Samad said, "Especially since worshipping the living is forbidden."

I said, "With the exception of one!"

Then a new group arrived with something that looked like a canopied litter, but shaped like a pyramid, draped in black, and with a bouquet of flowers on the front. We lit a cigarette. Someone handed us a page of poetry from the poet of such-and-such a neighborhood in Tehran. Here's a couplet from that poem:

The champions of the world were powerless in your fist,
What a shame it is that fortune brought you back to dust.

Then a distant friend arrived, said hello, and whispered in my ear, "Since yesterday, three persons have committed suicide. One in a hospital with a rope made from a sheet..." and left. I announced the news for everyone aloud. Silence. The first young man said, "You mean it has had a precedent even from two-thousand five-hundred years ago?"

I said, "Yes. The death of Siyavash." Then, silence.

Then I "climbed the pulpit," still standing on an unknown grave.

"In --- societies it's always like this. They kill the Siyavashes and the Sohrabs because they can't tolerate them. Then they recite lamentations after their deaths. Is it not true that Siyavash was something like an athlete? That he passed through water and fire? And what happened in the end?... Now we have only the mourning of him at his death, not his joy and exuberance while he lived... And other things of this sort..."

Then the sound of al-rahman [the merciful] rose from the loudspeaker. And we scattered and returned. And there was the bitterness of that spectacle and that headless crowd that at the end didn't even have the voice of a loudspeaker as its point of concentration. And a crowd, at that, whom we have accustomed to dictation; whose greatest sense of adventure is to climb a wall, or to sit at the edge of a low clay wall and view the graveyard, or to test the durability of Iranian tomb-vaults; and more important than all that, to flatter itself into contentment with the legends it creates. One was saying they've poisoned him with "barbiturate" (or barbi-torah?), the name of a poison. Another was saying they've strangled him. And yet another, that they've beaten him to death and then dragged his body into the hotel. Of that crowd, not one, not even for a moment, considered the possibility of suicide. After all, to have been a "world champion" and to have compensated in your "being" for the individual and social "non-being" of others, and then to have killed yourself? How could a common, powerless, and frightened man who saw the daily deterioration of his own self be compensated for in a meaningful existence, the strength of body, the fame of this native of Khani Abad — who never turned his back on his own class, this essence of body's strength who said "no" to the supreme power of his time, who did not become a Namju or Sha'ban or Habibi — how could this common and humble man believe that he had committed suicide? And anyway, isn't this folkloric legend-making a defensive method for the common man on the street to preserve his petrified personality in the face of dominating oppression and to remain hopeful? Siyavash and Sohrab have their own places. In this hierarchy we even have the heroic master butcher, or the leader of that sect who went into a cask of nitric acid, or the one who disappeared, or the other who ascended to heaven.

And what am I do to now? How am I to believe that Samad — who took the responsibility of fulfilling all obligations to his mother tongue by himself; who, after being discouraged by us, his older peers, and because of his own hatred of the "better-than-ourselves," finally took refuge with the children; who eventually despaired of having his *Alphabet* published because of all the "methodology" games they played on him, pretending to be "learned", promising that they would convert his book for adults, and always insisting on flaunting the letters *heh* and *mim* of his *Alphabet* through *mah* [moon] and *mah banu* [lady moon] in the children's faces — that same Samad is dead? And now that he's dead, would it suffice simply to say *la ilaha illa Allah*?! Even when Nima died, I was too grieved to eulogize. Now we must mourn in our agony for this younger brother and eulogize him? And anyway, how many Samads do we have? And would it suffice to do the "modern" thing and instead of crying in the sorrow of his death or dyeing one's beard with henna (and God knows I don't even have a beard!), to cry over the Karbala of Vietnam?... No, it's no good. Now it's better if I, at forty-five or six years of age, with a great deal of haughty airs and knowledge — though in a common way the most common of men — and as sceptical as any heretic you may imagine, instead of mourning this younger brother's death or carrying a cane, start a rumour that Samad, just like that *Little Black Fish*, has made his way through Aras to the sea so that he may reappear one day. After all, he has entered the water in the Khoda Afarin [lord creator] area, and he has entered the Aras! This separating sickle, this bisector of one culture and one language. You see, I had known that these names were as sacred to Samad as Medina had been to that older brother.

Translation by Leonardo P. Alishan,
University of Utah

16

EPILOGUE

In this final section, there are two translations. First is the brief concluding chapter of Al-e Ahmad's famous polemic essay *Gharbzadegi* [Weststruckness] (1962, 1964). Another chapter from *Gharbzadegi* is translated in "Iranian Education and the University," selection 13. The two published complete translations of *Gharbzadegi*, one a collaboration by John Green and Ahmad Alizadeh (1980) and the other by Paul Sprachman (1982), have been consulted in the preparation of the new translation of the last chapter here.

The second part of this epilogue presents the views of Shamsoddin Al-e Ahmad concerning his older brother's death as published in the cover story and interview on Al-e Ahmad in *Javan*, no. 27 (15 Tir 1979). Shams's views are particularly interesting in light of the insistence of Jalal's widow Simin Daneshvar, e.g., in "Ghorub-e Jalal" [Jalal's Dusk], *Arash*, no. 31 (Sept./Oct. 1981), that her husband died a natural death.

———————————

It's time now for me to put my pen down. Let me conclude, therefore with a few words about some prominent writers and with a prediction-like statement that isn't a prediction but rather the inevitable end of the road down which we and humanity are being lead.

The late French writer Albert Camus has a book called *The Plague*. It may be his masterpiece. It's the story of a city in North Africa which is visited by bubonic plague, who knows from where or why. Just like a sort of fate. Perhaps from the sky itself. At first, diseased and terrified mice pour out of their holes and appear in the alleyways, pathways, and streets. And in the course of a single day, every available garbage can is filled to the brim with their small corpses, each with a spot of blood at the corner of its mouth. And then the people get sick and get sick and get sick and then die and die and die. It reaches the point where the sounds of the hearses don't cease for a second. And it becomes necessary for people's corpses to be taken from their relatives by force, to be covered with lime and buried. The city is perforce quarantined, and all its citizens, with its plague-ridden walls, search for something or other. Some seek a treatment for the plague. Others hunt for a place to escape to. Some seek refuge in drugs. Still others seek to take advantage of the situation. In such a city, besides the dominance of death and helpless human efforts to escape it — and the sorrow that hangs like dust in the air — what strikes the eye more than anything else is that the presence of the plague, that demon of death, has merely speeded up the pace of everyone's footsteps along that route he or she was previously travelling. Whether right or wrong, whether moral or immoral, the presence of the plague not only failed to deter people from their wanted paths, but even flung them at a run along those same paths.

Just like us who are striken with the plague of *gharbzadegi*. Merely the pace of our affliction has speeded up.

When *The Plague* appeared, some critics (the ones on the right) said that Camus had represented Russian society through the allegory of the plague-striken city. Other critics (those on the left) said that he had planted the seeds of the Algerian Revolution in the book. And others said many other things I don't recall and don't think are pertinent... But I myself, not because of these opinions, but to discover the writer's basic message, undertook a translation of the book. And by the time a third of the translation was finished, I understood, that is I perceived the writer's message. And once the point to *The Plague* became apparent to me, I abandoned the translation project. I saw that in Camus' view the plague represented "machinism." This killer of beauty and poetry and humanity and the sky.

Sometime later, the play called *Rhinoceros* by the Frenchman Eugene Ionesco came out. Once again there's a city and its people. And all of them are living their daily lives without a care. Suddenly an illness spreads through the city. Note that like *The Plague*, once again it's a matter of a contagious disease. And what is this disease? Turning into a rhinoceros! First there's a fever, then a horn grows out of the forehead. And then the power to speak turns into the power to roar like an animal, and then the skin becomes thick, and so on. And eveyone gets it: housewives, neighborhood grocers, bank presidents, so-and-so's lover, and the rest. And all of them take to the streets and trample down the city and civilization and beauty. This time, of course, there was no need to translate the book in order to understand what the writer was saying (although as it turned out, I did it). But I always wanted to show in a commentary to a Persian translation how our honorable fellow Iranians likewise are day by day heading toward becoming rhinoceroses, which is the final resolution in the confrontation with the machine.

Then just recently (1961) in Tehran, I saw the movie *The Seventh Seal*. The work of the Swedish director Ingmar Bergman, a filmmaker from the northernmost reaches of the Western world, a man from the region of polar nights. The movie is set in the Middle Ages in another plague-stricken land. A knight has returned to his homeland from the Crusades tired and beaten and dejected. The point is here. He has returned from the Crusades where he never found truth because he saw in the Holy Lands those very things that today his Western descendants see in the colonized world of the East and Africa. And in contrast with today's Europeans, this knight did not come searching for oil and spices and silk. He came searching for truth. And absolute truth at that. That is today, he wanted to see and touch God in the Holy Lands of Palestine. Exactly like Christ's disciples who, because they thought they had seen God, trumpeted the Christian gospel in the four corners of the world.

This Swedish knight who came from the region of long polar nights to the land of the sun's blinding brightness was searching for God. However, instead of God, he found Satan in front of him every step of the way. Sometimes as a chess opponent, sometimes in the guise of a cleric. And always with the visage of the angel of death Ezra'il who had scattered the seeds of the plague in that land and was now reaping human souls. And in the days when our knight returned weary from his search for truth, the church was describing the torments of hell and the day of judgment, soon to come. Hints that once the age of faith comes to an end, there is an age of torment. When the age of belief ends, the age of experimentation begins. And experimentation likewise leads to the atomic bomb. These are Bergman's hints to us. Or my interpretation of them.

And now, not as an Easterner but just like a Moslem of the first generation who believed in divine revelation and who believed that before his or her own death he or she would be a spectator of the resurrection of the human race on the plains of Judgment, I see that Albert Camus, Eugene Ionesco, Ingmar Bergman, and many other artists, all of them from that very world of the West, are the harbingers of this very resurrection. All of them have washed their hands of the outcome of human activity. Sarte's Erostrate draws a gun with eyes closed on people in the street. And Nabokov's hero drives a car right at people. And Meursault, *The Stranger*, kills man merely because of the intensity of the sun's heat. These fictional outcomes, all of them, are reflections of the actual eventuality of the human race. Humanity that must surely put on rhinoceros skins if it doesn't want to be crushed under machines. And I see these story endings as warnings about humanity's final hour: the hydrogen bomb in the hand of the machine demon (if we don't capture it and put it's spirit back into the bottle)...

* * * * * *

I saw him for the last time on the seventh-night memorial service for Khalil Maleki. I had sent Jalal a telegram giving him the news of Khalil's death. The next day we saw each other at Maleki's gravesite. Jalal was so distraught that he afterwards returned directly to Esalem. And several days later, they brought me the news of Jalal's death.

For me Jalal's death was unnatural and wholly unexpected. For me this death was premature. I couldn't believe that Jalal would this soon be in the clutches of death. Jalal succumbed to outside forces... But as for by means of whom and what this crime took place, I don't know, because Jalal had been in a sort of exile at Esalem for four months. And, within a radius of seven kilometers of his cottage, there wasn't a single living creature, except at the lumber mill, whose workers came regularly to see Jalal.

Ms. Daneshvar has also alluded to this. Among the workers who regularly came to see Jalal, there were two of them who stopped by every day. It is said that these two were dressed in workers' clothes but in fact were security officers at the factory. So, in addition, they were on the lookout for Jalal, as can be surmised from the fact that the lumber mill's managers were two security police colonels...

Two days before Jalal's death occurred, five or six youths who appeared to be tourists and mountain climbers pitched a tent about four or five hundred meters from Jalal's cottage and camped there. Then, naturally, they took a look around and approached Jalal. Well, it's Jalal Al-e Ahmad! And they expressed great surprise. They talked, went to the sea together, went swimming, came back. But that afternoon when Jalal's death occurred — these young men were around in the morning, and in the late afternoon there wasn't a trace of them left!

When I got to Esalem, I saw Jalal laid out in his final sleep. I put my hand on his forehead. It was cold. But his hair underneath my hand was alive. We went and brought a physician. He, in turn, wrote on the death certificate that death had occurred as a result of a heart attack. When we got Jalal's corpse back to Tehran, we took him to the mortuary.

One large blood stain the size of an ashtray had soaked through the shroud on his nose... This is a symptom of a blow to the head. Such bleeding does not occur of its own accord — the capillaries would have to have burst under pressure for blood to flow from the nose... Furthermore, our cousin who had personally washed Jalal's body and placed it in the grave told us there was a swelling at the back of Jalal's head. When he was about to wrap the shroud around the head, he noticed this swelling, this lump. Also, Dr. Shaykh, the family physician who was a classmate of Jalal's and an old friend and who always monitored Jalal's physical condition, believed that Jalal had not exhibited any symptoms that might lead to a heart attack. Well, with all this information from witnesses and those close to Jalal, how can one believe that Jalal left this world with a natural death?...

...They couldn't let a shrewd person like Jalal loose on his own. They had threatened him many times. Now that I'm saying these things, my aim is that if one day people here and there should turn up information relating to Jalal's death, I also want to be informed so that the mystery of Jalal's death, like the deaths of [Gholamreza]

Takhti and Samad [Behrangi], might be cleared up. These three were people who influenced their own times. These three were movers of strata and classes in their own society. A society that the Pahlavi government and SAVAK wanted to turn into an island of stability. There it was necessary to silence obtrusive people. With inducements if they could. Or a position in an office or ministry with perquisites and pay raises. Or they'd attract them with dance halls and clubs and stables like the Chattanooga cabaret and... and keep them occupied. And if not they'd put him on the proverbial leash or exile him. Like His Excellency Imam Ayatollah Khomeini or like Khalil Maleki. They merely tied his hands and foot and imprisoned him in his own house and at his own expense. Why, because Maleki was known among world socialists — his friends either were presidents of republics or held high-ranking government positions, and SAVAK couldn't do away with him all at once.

SAVAK officials once told Jalal, "Don't think we'll kill you so that you can become a martyr or put you in jail so that you can become famous. You'll see that while you're walking along a sidewalk, a truck whose brakes don't work will drive onto the sidewalk and... And the first person who will hear the news will be Mr. [Prime Minister] Hoveyda. Also, we'll bury your corpse in Reza Shah's mausolemn..."

And Jalal, the combatant and master of discourse, our *sayyed* Jalal was martyred. The Sabetis [of SAVAK] wanted to occasion a quiet tragic accident in the style of the Mafia. And they did it. Just as they had said they would in their visit with our *sayyed*. Our martyred *sayyed*.

Translation by the editor

GLOSSARY

This glossary provides a brief explanation of selected names and places and attempts to define the most common use of each term or the meaning which the term has in this book. For further information consult the various references cited at the beginning of each selection [General Editor's Note].

Names

Abolfazl (Hazrat-e Abbas)
The younger brother of Imam Hosayn who was killed in Karbala, Iraq, along with seventy-two others. The mention of his name is a common expression of beseechment in Iran (See Imam Hosayn, below).

Akhavan Sales, Mehdi (b. 1928)
Born and raised in Mashhad, Akhavan Sales is considered by some critics as the greatest living poet of Iran.

'Alam, Asadollah
A wealthy landlord from Birjand and one of the late Shah's closest friends and confidants who was appointed Prime Minister in 1962 and played an active role in supressing the June 5, 1963 uprising inspired by Ayatollah Khomeini. He died in a New York hospital of an illness prior to the 1979 revolution.

'Ali Akbar
The eldest son of Imam Hosayn who was martyred at the age of eighteen in Karbala, Iraq in 680 A.D. According to some Shi'ah scholars, Imam Hosayn was present as his son was dying and mourned him as he spoke his last words. Some believe that he was the first Shi'ah martyr [See Mullah Hosayn Va'ez Kashefi, *Rowzat al-Shohada*, (Tehran: Eslamieh, 1970), pp. 336-342.]

'Aliyeh Khanom
The wife of poet Nima Yushij and the daughter of Mirza Nasrollah Esfahani (Malek ol-Motakalemin, a prominent figure in the 1906 Persian Constitutional Revolution).

Baraheni, Reza
A leading poet and social critic, Baraheni became active in anti-Pahlavi movements and subsequently arrested. After serving a brief

term in jail, he was released and exiled to the United States. His major English work *The Crowned Cannibals* was published in 1977. It described the general state of oppression in Iran. He is a member of *Hezb-e Kargaran Socialist* [Socialist Workers Party], a Trotskyite group in Iran.

Behruz

Reference to Behruz Dehqani a close friend of Samad Behrangi and a collaborator in a number of literary and folkloric projects. After Samad's death he became a militant revolutionary, later to be arrested and executed by the Shah's regime. His sister, Ashraf, is an active member of the *Churikhay-e Fadu'y-e Khalq* (minority branch) carrying on an armed struggle against the government of the Islamic Republic of Iran somewhere in Kurdestan.

Bestami, Bayazid (d. 874 A.D.)

One of the most celebrated Sufis of the third century A.H.

Dashti, 'Ali

A writer and newspaper editor who cooperated with the Pahlavi regime and was appointed to the Senate by the late Shah.

Davar, 'Ali Akbar

Minister of Finance in 1932 who was instrumental in the negotiations between the former Anglo-Persian Oil Company and the government of Iran under Reza Shah. He later committed suicide.

Ebn-e Babuyeh

A Moslem scholar and teacher whose place of burial is the site of a cemetery where many famous Iranians are buried.

Habibi, Gholam'ali

A world champion wrestler who cooperated with the Shah's regime and subsequently became a member of the *Majlis* [Parliament].

Hedayat, Sadeq (1903-51)

Iran's most famous and controversial twentieth century author, journalist and prose writer. He is best remembered for his piece of fiction, *Buf-e Kur* [The Blind Owl]. Committed suicide in Paris.

Hoveyda, [Amir Abbas]

Iranian prime minister for thirteen years, he was removed from office by the Shah in July, 1977 in the face of mounting opposition and was appointed minister of court. Still in jail when the Shah fled Iran, Hoveyda was captured by the revolutionaries and executed after a brief and hastily arranged trial.

Imam Hosayn

The third imam of the Shi'ah who was killed in a battle against Yazid (son of Mo'aviyeh the founder of Umayyed dynasty) in Karbala, Iraq, in 680 A.D. He is considered to be the greatest Shi'ah martyr and the circumstances surrounding his death have evolved throughout Shi'i history into a symbol of resistance against tyranny and despotism.

Imamzadeh Davoud

Imamzadeh (or Emamzadeh) literary means "the son or a decendent of an Imam." In popular usage, however, it refers to the shrine or the mausoleum of an imamzadeh whose name it bears. There are many such holy shrines scattered around Iran which are visited and revered by local residents.

Imamzadeh Hashem

The shrine of Hashem, a descendant of an imam (See also Imamzadeh Davoud).

Jamalzadeh, Mohammad 'Ali (b. 1895)

Born in Isfahan and the son of Sayyed Jamal Va'ez (a leading clerical constitutionalist from Isfahan), Jamalzadeh is considered by many experts as the leader in modern Persian prose fiction. He is the author of several novels and many short stories. He currently resides in Switzerland.

Kasravi, Ahmad (1890-1946)

Scholar, historian, journalist and essayist, Kasravi was born in Azarbayjan and grew up during the Constitutional Revolution. A one-time student of Shi'ah theology, he later became an outspoken critic of the clerical establishment. He was assassinated in 1946 by a member of the fundamentalist group Fada'yan-e Islam.

Khanlari, Parviz

A writer and a poet, he was the former head of the Cultural Foundation of Iran and the editor of the literary journal, *Sokhan.*

Maham

Once the mayor of Tehran in early 1960's, he became known and ridiculed for his obsession to build fountains as part of his beautification project for the city of Tehran.

Maleki, Khalil (d. 1969)

One of the original founders of the Tudeh Party who later broke away in 1945 and established his own political party named *Niruy-e Sevvom* [Third Force]. An astute socialist thinker and a brilliant theoretician, he was the editor of *Elm-o Zendegi* magazine.

Namju, Mahmud

A champion weightlifter who endorsed the Shah's regime.

Naser Khosrow (Qobadiyani Marvazi), (1004-88 A.D.)

A well-known 11th century Iranian poet and writer who became a convert to the Isma'ilieh (Seveners) creed in Egypt under Fatimid rule. He returned to Khorasan to popularize his creed but met with opposition from the authorities. He eventually settled in a village in the mountains of Badakhshan where he died. He is well remembered for his *Safarnameh* [The Travelogue].

Reza Shah

The founder of Pahlavi dynasty in 1926 and the father of the late deposed shah. He was forced to abdicate the throne by the Allied in 1941 and died in South Africa in exile.

Sabeti, [Parviz]

Also nicknamed "the pupils of the Shah's eyes," Sabeti rose in the ranks of SAVAK to become the second most important official in the security organization during the Shah's rule. He was an expert in dealing with the intellectuals and was the Shah's most trusted civilian in the SAVAK. He held frequent television interviews with the intellectuals who had been tortured and forced to recant. He has fled Iran after the revolution.

Sa'edi, Gholam Reza

A prominent Iranian playwright and fiction writer who is also an amateur ethnographer and a professional psychiatrist. An activist against the Shah's regime, he is best known for his filmscript, *The Cow*.

Shah Abdol'azim

A Shi'ah holy man buried in a shrine in the city of Ray to the south of Tehran.

Sha'ban [Ja'fari] "The Brainless"

The leader of at least two pro-Shah and anti-Mosaddeq mobs for which he was handsomely rewarded by the Shah's regime. He fled Iran after the 1979 revolution.

Shamlu, Ahmad (b. 1925)

Also known by his pen name, A. Bamdad, Shamlu has been a prominent literary figure in Iran. Since the death of Nima Yushij in 1960, he has been an elder statesman among modernist, engage' Iranian poets.

Siyavash

The son of Kaykavus, a king in ancient Persia, appears in Iranian epic poet Ferdowsi's *Shahnameh* [The Book of Kings]. Purity and valor are his main characteristics, both shown by his willingness to walk through fire in order to prove his innocence. He was later killed by Afrasiyab, the evil Turanian king, with whom he had taken refuge because of his father's haughtiness and obstinate demands.

Sohrab

One of the characters in Ferdowsi's *Shahnameh* [the Book of Kings], Sohrab is the son Tahmineh is carrying when Rostam, a Hercules-type Iranian national hero, leaves her and returns to Iran. In his early youth Sohrab decides to search for his father. They meet, however, as foes, and fate helps their identities to remain unknown to each other. After Rostam mortally wounds his own son, he discovers only too late that he has killed his own offspring. His grief and lamentations are among the most heartrendering verses of the *Shahnameh*.

Tabari, Ehsan

One of the founders of the Tudeh Party and the party's theoretician. He lives in Tehran and is active in the party's politics.

Zahra, Fateme al-

The only surviving daughter of Prophet Mohammad who became wife of Imam 'Ali, the first Shi'ah imam.

Terms and Places

ahya

A night-long prayer rituals observed by the devout Shi'ahs particularly in connection with the death of Imam 'Ali.

Akhund

A low-ranking Shi'ah clergy. Also used discourteously to refer to the clergy.

Amiz

An abbreviated form for *Aqa Mirza*.

Aqa

Persian word meaning "Sir" or "Mister". Also a courteous way of addressing the clergy.

aqameh

Literary meaning "to stand up straight," it is part of the ritual of daily prayers, *namaz*, when the person stands before God and recites the words of the prayer.

'araq

Iranian vodka distilled from raisins. Also a generic name for any type of vodka.

Aras River

The river which forms the border between Iran and the Soviet Union to the northwest. The river basin is formed like a sickle, the blade facing the Soviet Union and the handle touching the Caspian Sea.

azan

Call to prayer.

chador

A shapeless garb made of different color material worn by Iranian women to cover their body from the sight of strange men.

Dar ol-Fonun

The first Iranian institute of arts and sciences established by Prime Minister Amir Kabir in 1851. Today it remains as one of Tehran's famous high schools.

Daqyanus

Decius.

Dehkharqan

A village near Tabriz, the capital of east Azarbayjan.

Democrat Farqasi

A political party established by Ja'far Pishevari in the province of Azarbayjan in December, 1945 during the Soviet occupation of the region. The party proclaimed the Autonomous Republic of Azarbayjan and received the backing of the Soviet government. The movement was crushed by the central government once the Soviet Army evacuated the region.

Falak ol-Aflak

A prison in the city of Korram Abad in Lurestan in the western part of Iran.

Joshan-e Kabir

A prayer recited during the blessed month of Ramazan.

Kamel

A prayer recited during the month of Ramazan.

Karbala

A city in Iraq where Imam Hosayn and seventy-two of his companions were killed in 680 A.D. It is the site of one of the holiest

Shi'i shrines.

Karaj

A small city to the north of Tehran and the site of Iran's largest agricultural college.

khambaji

An abbreviation for *Khanom baji* [lady sister].

Khani Abab

A poor neighborhood in the south Tehran district where Gholam Reza Takhti, Iran's world champion wrestler, was born.

Khanom

Persian word meaning "lady."

Khoda Afarin

A town located approximately two-hundred and forty-five kilometers northeast of Tabriz on the banks of the Aras River.

Khosrow Shah

A village twenty-eight kilometers southeast of Tabriz.

korsi

A traditional Iranian method of keeping warm during the winter months, a *korsi* is made of a wooden frame looking like a square dining table with short legs. It is covered all around with quilts and blankets under which a brazier of hot coal is placed for heating the legs in the winter.

kucheh

A narrow alley way connecting streets in the cities.

la ilaha illa Allah

"There is no deity, but Allah," is the first part of the Creed of the Moslem. This phrase is followed by *Mohammadan Rasul ullah* [Mohammad is the Prophet of Allah]. The first part of the creed appears in the Koran, Chapter XLVII, verse 21, and the second part in Chapter XLVIII, verse 29.

The first part is known as the *nafy* [rejection] and *esbat* [affirmation], and in Iran it is often recited in the moments of distress and sorrow.

Mamqan

A village near Tabriz.

Manaf

The name of a pagan idol in pre-Islamic Arabia. Al-e Ahmad's reference to it is meant to indicate a deaf and dumb audience; a statue-like unsympathetic listener.

Marwa
A mound near Mecca connected to *Safa* by a street named *Mas'a*. It is a sacred place visited by the *hajj* pilgrims.

Mas'a
See *sa'y*.

miqat
The term is applied to the times of prayer and the places where those who enter the *haram* are bound to put on the *ihram* [See: *Shorter Encyclopaedia of Islam,* edited by H. A. R. Gibb and J. H. Kramers, (Leiden: E. J. Brill, 1953), p. 379.]

Nakir and Monkar
Names of two angels who, according to the Shi'ah belief popularized by the mullahs, interrogate the dead person in his tomb on the first night after burial. The person, it is said, will be asked several questions about his belief in God, the Prophet Mohammad, the first Imam and the five pillars of Shi'ah doctrine. If he is unable to respond correctly, he will be struck on the head by a burning bludgeon sending him directly to hell.

National Front
A coalition of secular and religious opposition groups and parties formed in 1949 by the late Prime Minister Mohammad Mosaddeq to enforce the nationalization of the oil industry. The party remains active as of today although the original composition has changed.

Nishabur
A city in Khorasan to the northeast of Iran and the birthplace of Omar Khayyam.

paludeh
Sweet ice cream-like desert containing starch jelly in the form of thin fibers served with lemon juice or sour cherry syrup.

Qazvin
A city approximately 120 kilometers to the northwest of Tehran.

Ramazan
The ninth month of the Moslem lunar calendar which is also the month of fasting.

rowzeh
The recitation of verses concerning the martyrdom of the Shi'i imams, particularly Imam Hosayn.

Safa
A mound at Mecca and one of the sacred places visited by the pilgrims during the *hajj* ceremonies.

Samat

A prayer recited during the month of Ramazan.

Sa'y

Part of the *hajj* ceremonies. The pilgrim after performing the circumambulation of the *Kaaba* and drinking from the water of Zamzam proceeds to cover the course between *Safa* and *Marwa* at a slow pace. *Mas'a* is the street connecting the two mounds. A *sa'y* consists of seven such courses.

Sefid Rud

A river originating in the mountains of Chehel Cheshmeh [Forty Springs] in Kurdestan and, like the Aras River, flows into the Caspian Sea.

sharbat

A thick syrup made of various fruit juices, diluted with water and served over ice during the summer months.

Shemiran

Once a small resort village to the north of Tehran, it is now a small city where many wealthy Iranians live. It is known for its temporate climate and many recreational areas which offer a refuge to thousands during the hot summer months.

sofreh

Table cloth traditionally spread on the floor. People sit around it when eating.

tasbih

Persian prayer beads.

Third Force (Niruy-e Sevvom)

A political party with socialistic-nationalistic ideals established by Khalil Maleki (see Maleki, Khalil).

Yush

A village in the Alburz Mountains northeast of Tehran which is the birthplace of the poet, Nima Yushij.

za'ifeh

Literary meaning "the weak one" it is a popular phrase used by the uneducated and traditional males to refer to women.

zekr

A prayer recited in remembrance of someone.

zendiq

An Arabic word meaning "atheist," "dualist," or "sadducee."